BASIC POLITICS OF MOVEMENT SECURITY

A TALK ON SECURITY
with J. Sakai

May 2013

G20 REPRESSION
& INFILTRATION
IN TORONTO:
An Interview
With Mandy Hiscocks

reprinted from
Upping The Anti #14

KER
SPL
EBE
DEB
2014

Basic Politics of Movement Security
Kersplebedeb 2014

A Talk on Security © J. Sakai 2013

G20 Repression & Infiltration in Toronto:
An Interview With Mandy Hiscocks © Upping the Anti 2012

ISBN: 978-1-894946-52-0

First printing
This edition © Kersplebedeb 2014

        Kersplebedeb Publishing and Distribution
        CP 63560
        CCCP Van Horne
        Montreal, Quebec
        Canada H3W 3H8

email: info@kersplebedeb.com
web: www.kersplebedeb.com
        www.leftwingbooks.net

FOREWORD
FOREWORD

This is months after the talk, and sitting down with the transcript from a recording made me smile. Often it reads so rough, as though sentences were jumbled in a torrent through the mixer. Originally, the plan was to use the talk as a kind of skeleton and warmup exercise, and build up to a proper paper or article. But, finally, i decided against that, and instead opted to leave much of the talk transcript in for print as a record of a live event on this subject. Also, this better frames the group discussion, which was too sharp to leave out. Comrades were unusually thoughtful. Many people had clearly been really thinking about security and wanted a chance to discuss it in some focused setting with other comrades. So hopefully some of that's been saved.

A poet once noted, "Art being bartender is never drunk." Just so there was an agenda in giving this talk, as every political act has agency, tactics, and so forth. Many warnings on security that i've heard have been pretty formalistic. You know, lists of things not to do, mostly. My goal was to short-circuit that for now, and talk about the real life struggle and politics behind security as an area of struggle.

As part of that, i didn't tell people at the meeting but i had steered wide to avoid technical discussion. When security comes up, one problem is a tendency of some guys fascinated with technique and especially technology, to run away with the discussion. This has a good side, for sure, but to me what the movement needs first is to work out our political understanding of security.

In the Q&A, there was one comrade who asked a serious question about how we deal with all the compromises and trade-offs involved in doing security. Such as the benefit of computer encryption for our emails and messages versus the daily added work of using it. i refused to answer, in part because such questions could only be discussed with practical examples which would involve laborious back and forth, too much for a short public meeting. And i was personally simply too tired physically at that point to deal with it seriously as it deserved. His question was left in, though, so that readers could think over his point.

Even here, though, politics shines the farthest light. When a comrade once was offering me the favor of installing an "unbreakable" encryption program on my dusty old Apple, without his ever thinking about it a number of political decisions were involved. Was this so that i could have "sensitive" messaging and say dangerous things to other comrades without fear of the state? If so, that means i should be willing to risk prison for using that "security" measure. Prison or death for my comrades as well as myself. Betting that this particular technology is "unbreakable" or can never be defeated.

Of course, our encryption does not have to be cracked to be overcome. The weakest link is the enduser. Any encryption does no good if your laptop itself has had remote control covertly installed on it, or if it is physically bugged. Journalists whose life's work depends on repelling state computer surveillance—such as those who worked with NSA leaker Edward Snowden—never let their laptops leave their sight. They always had the machines physically with them. It's a strict regimen, for sure.

If in five or ten years NSA or a band of brilliant hackers in Uruguay does succeed in cracking that code, NSA won't be nice enough to warn us. They'll want us to go right on blathering away telling them everything. Plus NSA has by their own admission saved every single email message ever sent globally since the birth of the internet, so if they ever crack that supposedly eternally invincible code someone's ass would be grass. Hmm, that's a lot to risk just for the privilege of talking indiscreetly. Nothing wrong with having computer encryption or using word substitution code in telephone calls or whatever, but am for always being discreet and careful too.

And on a deeper level, have to question the whole idea of trade-offs and compromises as a "problem". Know what people mean by this, and have thought it myself many times. But it's there all the time in life, ordinary life, not just in this rarified slice called politics. Using condoms, isn't that an annoying trade-off or compromise ? Or having faster food instead of an hour's work of home cooked meal because we're kinda beat after work? Or … you can fill in the blanks. If we look at it in a zen political way, though, there is no such thing. No compromises, no trade-offs. That is only an illusion our mind creates in its confusion. If you really understand a situation, fully comprehend it, then you know precisely what you have to do. You don't resent it or question it or wish you could only do half of it, because it's the right action then whatever it is .

Called this an "informal talk" because it isn't based on a book and wasn't built on any research. Just talked about this subject off the cuff, as we might do any evening with comrades. So this version went through some steps in addition to the usual editorial cleanup. A number of comments or explanations were added afterwards, and these are usually marked by being in a grey box. And in a few places examples were moved around or replaced by others which much better showed the point i was hoping to make.

i was afraid to do this talk, because traditionally it is never done (except in closed members only group educationals, which i've sometimes heard complaints about but never been in one myself). Never even seen a pamphlet or book on this subject. Obviously,there are good reasons not to publicly disclose your security work. Not sure what this is supposed to look like, so please just take this as a sharing. There are several things which should be clear in reading this, however.

This talk and its discussion that night only scratched the surface of how security should be understood and worked on. Many important things were not even mentioned. So don't worry, we haven't done all the work already, there's lots for you to do. And then there's the consumer product safety warning on the label—there isn't any. That is, the goal of security isn't to protect you personally, though it may help do that. The goal of security is to protect the movement itself, to let the larger struggle against capitalism move forward.

Finally, at the anarchist book fair last May in Montreal, someone handed me a copy of *Upping The Anti* and asked if i'd seen the latest issue. Really, hadn't even known it was coming out. The day after the security talk, finally got a chance to kick back and open the magazine and start checking it out. Almost swallowed my chewing tobacco. Near the end was an interview with Mandy Hiscocks on the state's repression of the G20 Toronto mass protests in 2010, done before she went into prison. If i had known about it before my talk, would have brought it up to discuss. This is some serious thinking over of what the state did and what the movement did in an intense political crunch in the imperial metropolis. Security in a "right now" type situation. While some comrades have seen her interview in *UTA* already, many comrades in the u.s. probably have missed it as i did. So Mandy Hiscocks is letting us reprint it here to further share her experience, spread her radical insights.

J.S.

The Politics of Security

a presentation by J. Sakai

Monday, May 27th, 6:30 pm

@ QPIRG Concordia
1500 deMaisonneuve W., rm. 204
(metro Guy-Concordia)

Wheelchair accessible

Whisper translation into French
Traduction chuchoté vers le français

Got questions? info@kersplebedeb.com

A TALK ON SECURITY
WITH J. SAKAI

This informal talk was originally given on May 27, 2013 in Montreal, as part of Festival of Anarchy.

i'm going to speak for a little while generally. Then i'm going to go more into security, and how state infiltration against the movement has worked. This is in the u.s., mostly, what i'm familiar with. And what its results were, and both the movement's successes and failures in terms of combating the security agencies. Kind of some of what really happened. And then we can have Q&A. Okay?

A lot of times when we think about security we're still kind of uneasy about it. It's kind of like this little box way off on the side. It's not part of how we think of our regular politics or struggles we're involved in. Maybe, to us it's kind of a little dirty, and something confusing. Not certain how we can relate to it as a question. And if we do try to relate to it and deal with it, then we suddenly discover that, "Darn, there's no *Security for Dummies*". You go to the bookshelf and there isn't a book. Because the tradition is, at least in the u.s. where i come from, that this is a question where knowledge is handed down and transmitted by word-of-mouth, kind of personally. So sometimes when there's a generational discontinuity, big gap in passing on of this. So that's one of the reasons i'm talking about it here.

i'm not an expert on security from some security commission. i'm not a professor. i have nothing against them, but that's not what i am. i'm not a professor who studied this for their lifetime and who writes books on it. i'm just a movement activist. And so i've been taught basic things that i'd like to pass some of it on. i've witnessed security successes against the state and security failures. i'd like to pass that on.

Security is an area that's essentially divided into two parts. The first is our attempt to understand, keep track of and spotlight police activity. Eventually at some points even penetrate the armor of state domestic security agencies. What traditionally has been called the "political police".

The second part, of course, is dealing with their attempts to infiltrate our movements and activities, gain information against us, jam things up, harm people—and don't make any mistake about it they're definitely into harming people. This is not the nice guys' club, no matter what they always say.

Forgot to say during the talk, that the security lit that has been available is usually about the more dramatic illegal or or underground work. Such as Victor Serge's often-reprinted classic on clandestine tactics to evade the Russian Czarist police. Or the 1980s Black Liberation Army pamphlet that's taking off from Serge's lessons, "Fooling" by Seldom Seen. They're good but not our greatest need, it isn't on that level that's the biggest problem. It's for security understanding about public mass movements, for ordinary groups, that operate more-or-less on a legal level. Since this is the origin, the entry point for almost all people and issues into rebellion. And if we can't make it work on this level, we sure can't do a more difficult level.

The key thing is, to start with—and it's the most basic understanding—security is not about being macho vigilantes or being super suspicious or having techniques of this or that. It's not some spy game. **Security is about good politics**. That's why it's so difficult. And it requires good politics from the movement as a whole. Not from some special body or leadership or commission—from the movement as a whole. This is demanded of us. It's part of the requirement to be a revolutionary, that you try to work on this.

When we say "good politics", well, what is that? Everybody will say they have good politics. So really this cannot be assumed. It absolutely has to be broken down. Or, as the congregation always shouts back at the Baptist preachers, *"Make it plain"*. So we're going to try and make it plain, as much as we can here.

First of all, good politics is not the ideology you may or may not have learned from reading a book of Marx or Proudhon or something like that. That's good, it's part of education, part of politics. But that's not sufficient. In terms of security, that and 2 bucks will get you a cup of coffee. That's about it.

Security demands a higher level of politics. A level of practice and experience, in all three of its aspects. It demands individual experience, collective experience, and historical experience, melded into one knowledge. And that may be a lot for us, but it's just part of life, it's what's demanded of us, to do this work.

You know, after all, if you think about it, it's like revolutionary zebras, a collective of them on the high savanna in Africa. They're always being stalked by predators. Well, how do they deal with that? They deal with it usually pretty handily. Because that's their terrain. They can read their terrain. The ripples on the grasses, all the information brought by the wind. They read that, they understand it.

The same with us when we struggle with capitalism. When we attack capitalist society—that area that we're on, that we're engaging them on, this is for that time our terrain. Part of the terrain is still theirs because this is still capitalism. A part of it is now ours because we made it so . And we have to be able to read that terrain, the constant ripples, changes in it, and understand what they mean, you know, in real life.

it's just like, when i came into the movement—had been around the movement from my early teen years, just cause i hung out with the small pack of nerds and leftovers in secondary school, and many were from movement families. But when i was 18, i joined a social-democratic organization which was pretty moderate and pretty worthless, really, but it was there and i was so glad to find other people to join with and do something political.

7

Within a year i met 4 people in the group or who came to its public meetings, who were agents. And this is not some case of rumors that they were said to be agents, they all sooner or later confessed to being agents. Okay? In each of the four cases i would not have thought they were agents. i was 18 years old, why would i have thought someone was a police agent? i wasn't thinking of that stuff. Someone quietly came up to me and said, "You know so and so is probably an agent, and this is why. You should listen to him, check it out. This is why we think he's an agent."

So, one guy, for example, clearly he'd gone to see a Hollywood movie or two about leftists or anarchists or something, and that's what his act was based on. He was a young college dropout, finding excitement by working for the FBI. So he had a dramatic pose, wore a beret and a black turtleneck sweater, and he smoked Gauloises, the French cigarette, like what he thought the Left Bank of Paris was like. The other thing is he always made these really angry-sounding speeches which were incomprehensible because he actually didn't have any politics, you know. He didn't have any good political points or bad political points, he didn't have any political points at all just about. He was peppering his speech with all kinds of words that he heard others use. The "dialectic" this, the "oppressor" that. It was just peppered in.

After awhile, i wasn't listening to him. i was just tuning him out. But when i was listening to him and he just didn't have any politics at all, that i could ascertain—so what the hell is he doing here? Then it dawned: Oh, *that's* why you think he might be a police agent! And the more experienced comrades didn't try to beat him up or anything, just made fun of him—and created a kind of bubble around him. Anything important wasn't discussed near him.

When we look at domestic security agencies, the political police (and it may be somewhat different in the u.s. than in Canada, my experience is all in the u.s. so i may be saying things that are really obvious as A-B-C to people in Canada and you know this all already and that's good, so i'm sorry if this is just old stuff), what we see is the regular police force always justifies political policing and domestic security persecutions as *i've never forgotten about that real unimportant police spy, in part because of a completely unrelated incident. Many years later, was sitting in on a small meeting as a gofer, just in case anyone wanted coffee or we had to go photocopy something. It was a bigshot Hollywood agent and her client, an actress named Angelina Jolie, trying to convince some prisoner support workers who had been in the news lately, to sign over the rights to their life stories without any payment. Usual capitalistic rip-off biz. But what i was thinking about all the while was: "Don't i know her from somewhere? She's real familiar somehow." Which bothered me, since obviously i didn't know her. Then it hit me, damn, she's just like that police agent actor character was years ago. The mind is a funny thing, connects up things in unexpected ways. She also had a beret and a black turtleneck sweater on under her worn denim jacket, just like he did. His face had been rough, with like acne scars, and hers—now that i really looked at it—was all professionally made up to look off, a bit disfigured like she'd been in a factory accident or something. What crap, for a political meeting with the movement! And she was actually even crying at one point, weeping, saying impassioned but illogical things, trying to get over with her ripoff of our movement. Good try, rookie, but like him she was detected as phoney and politely repelled from our terrain.*

the normal outgrowth of their claimed attempts to be preventing mugging or having traffic accidents or whatever.

This is totally untrue of course. Instinctively we know it's untrue, but factually it's just completely untrue in several ways. First, obviously, because the everyday police are there primarily to protect capitalist property and maintain that order in general. While the political police are a part of that, but more narrowly are a counter-insurgency police targeted against political enemies of the state, and in particular dissident groups of the colonized peoples and classes. That is, we could see them as an intelligence police for the oppressors in our permanent internal class war.

Let me use an example which may not seem to connect up for awhile. So bear with me:

Once i was on federal government probation for a couple of years for a protest they didn't like, and by "coincidence" my probation officer happened to be the commanding officer of the 113th US Army Military Intelligence Detachment, which is a reserve unit. And his supervising my probation consisted of every few weeks he would appear unannounced at my job, in front of everybody haul me out of work, march me out actually in front of everybody. Put me in the lobby or the hallway and subject me to his, what he obviously thought was his very slick psychological intimidation and brain washing. And it's kind of gross, and i'm going to mention it only for two reasons: one to show what they really are like and secondly because the u.s. military are still using these exact same tactics that they were trying to use on me, which were really simple and ugly:

He would say, basically, "You know, I'm your friend and here you are, you know you're a young guy in trouble and you know you just aren't having fun in life and here's why," and then he would start with all the stories of all the Asian women he'd used and how in Korea the lowliest G.I. in his unit had 2 women that sexually serviced him full-time and he of course had many more being the big officer and you know the life you could have if you came over to his side, you know, and became a real man, which i wasn't. Be a real man and you could go around the world raping women, forcing women into brothels and so forth.

So this is kind of wacky. Why would he be saying this dumb crap? And then i realized: well, firstly he's trying to obviously mess with my mind. You know, week after week, we would have this little conversation. First of all if he could get me to break, like, "Okay, i can't take this anymore, and i'm going to punch you out." Well, then, hold it, then I'm in jail for another coupla years. Well, he wouldn't mind that. Or, he keeps emphasizing the thing that, see, he's a real man. i'm not a real man, of course, because i don't have these things, i'm not doing these things that real imperialist men do. So he kept saying to me that i could either hate myself because i'm not a real man, and this may sound funny but this works sometimes on young guys. Or, i could somehow find his spiel attractive because he always said, you know you could have all this. You don't have to have your miserable life, you could have this glamorous military life; you could be in in some Asian country with all the local women you want or if you like another country to have women in, you can do this too.

This sounds unbelievably stupid and crude, and it was. Well, do you know, they're still doing that to this very day. The u.s. army has things that they use. It's unofficial of course. They will disavow it. But they always use it. For example, specially against Asian guys. So you have an 18-year-old Asian volunteer in the army who was stupid enough to join anyway knowing he was going to go to Afghanistan to kill civilians or get his ass blown off. Anyhow, so he's there and the typical thing is, the training sergeant will walk by him and he's in the barracks looking at home pictures. You're lonesome and you're homesick and you're looking at home photos. And the Sgt. will come lean over your shoulder and will say "Oh, that's a nice looking girl, is that your sister?" and you'll say "Oh, yeah." The Sgt. says, "Yeah, I thought so, I fucked her when I was on leave" and then he walks away and says, "Next time I'm going to fuck your mother." So, of course maybe you can... once again, you can punch him out—well, a year or whatever in jail for you—or you can start hating yourself because you have to take this crap, or think you're not a man like he is.

The thing is what does this have to do with policing? With security? It turns out the 113th Military Intelligence detachment was part of the shadow government behind the Chicago Police Red Squad that was investigating and infiltrating the 1960s-70s antiwar movement. They and by implication larger military agencies, were selecting targets and guiding our local police. And in fact they got into a lot of trouble, this military intelligence detachment, because they weren't content with that and they started sending their own guys out to observe the movement, maybe sabotage it or whatever. Except they got caught doing it and that was kind of embarrassing, because the u.s. army wasn't supposed to be doing that in the city of Chicago. The cops are supposed to be doing it. The division of labor for bourgeois legality purposes. **But when we say that political police are not just an outgrowth, an innocent extension of local policing, right, this can't be emphasized too much.**

Like New York City, in the late '60s the New York City Police Department decided it had to get rid of its Red Squad, because traditionally the subversive squad in the New York City police

After the meeting i got questions about whether we could better define the difference between police in general and the political police? Since many of us can see that all the police patrolling the occupied neo-colonial peoples in New York City or Los Angeles, for example, are pretty damn "political". You know, in middle-class "white" suburbs and expensive urban neighborhoods, most police work is about individual crimes with little of it lethal or even violent—you know, a car gets vandalized or something is stolen out of a garage or someone is drunk and disorderly. Completely different in the neo-colonial zones, where the cops are visibly uninterested in stopping the wholesale epidemic of burglary or muggings or rapes or killings, but only work to pressure youth away from of civilian life and into the drug trade and gunfights and prison.

In the talk i bent over backwards to emphasize the division between regular capitalist policing and the political police, because too many comrades assume that the political police are just some of their own familiar police but turned around to focus on them. Not true strategically. The political police may be similar people and similar uniforms but have of necessity a very different mindset and plans.

Having said that, we have to also recognize that the repressive arms of the state are steadily coming closer and closer to each other, becoming more like each other, as global capitalism develops and also homogenizes divided societies and cultures. Beat cops in neo-colonized communities who have always been an alien occupation force, now have to function as an adjunct to organized intelligence units. Just as police SWAT teams in the 1970s were only the initial cutting edge in the militarization of local police forces. Right after images of the killing of Osama bin Laden by the elite u.s. special ops commandos went worldwide, i also saw a newspaper photo of Brazilian police tactical officers leaving a favela of the poor they had invaded—and from the dark coveralls to the bulky loaded combat vests and military ballistic helmets and full-auto assault rifles on long slings, the two groups of u.s. elite commandos and Latin American police completely looked alike.

department was geared on investigating trade unions and all that old stuff that was really hot in 1920. Or was after the Communist Party or something Cold War that was dead as a doornail by then, and they weren't really keeping up with the times. So it became clear that the Red Squad had to be totally rebuilt. So u.s. intelligence—not city hall in New York—u.s. intelligence said, you know, New York is the major capital in reality, it's critical to us. When we see that the police department has a problem which is that they're a white settler police department representing a white settler government, ruling a city with a large colonial population of color that's increasingly getting rebellious. And they don't know what to do about it because they have these old-fashioned anti-subversive ideas.

So who has more expertise in a situation like theirs? Oh, those settler South Africans in Johannesburg!

So u.s. intelligence arranged for a team of counter-insurgency detectives from what was then named the South African Bureau of State Security (obviously called by the acronym "BOSS") in Johannesburg, i.e. the settler Afrikaner political police, to fly over to New York and to help be the big brothers, reorganizing, retraining, getting the New York City political police up to speed. To honor their Apartheid mentors, the N.Y.P.D. also officially named its own political police squad after them, also "B.O.S.S." It was their settler guys' little imperialist in-group joke, since their whole relationship was secret back then (the squad's name has been changed several times since then, naturally). Today the New York City political police, which is commanded by a former top CIA official, has branches all over the United States and in eleven foreign cities, including Toronto. It's a little far from New York City, but they clearly have their reasons to maintain that major investment in terms of what they're doing.

The difference between regular policing, capitalist crap as it is, and the political police is going to become apparent as we talk because there is an important difference. One of the things that's true about the political police throughout the capitalist world is that they're all different but also all "family" in the sense that they're descended, unbelievably as it is, from the Okhrana, the department for the protection of the public order of the Czarist government in late 19th-century Russia. Which was the first modern political police force under capitalism and was actually quite innovative. Its genetic makeup persists literally to this day inside political police almost everywhere.

So the Okhrana did the usual things you would think. They followed people, infiltrated groups, arrested people, blah blah, blah. But they actually also had a whole different strategic vision, which was really controversial inside that primitive Russian state. It's controversial actually today in most capitalist states, because there's a division in security between the people who in effect want to do accelerated or militarized policing— "Well, why can't we just arrest them all, just beat them up and shoot them, and put them in prison as much as we can, right, at every opportunity"—versus the people who actually usually end up running things, because to be honest they're smarter. They have an interesting view. They have our class understanding actually. They're just on the other side.

i was in a classified library once—a law enforcement library, with publications that would fill this room, and mostly none of us has ever seen these things because they're classified—reading a classified FBI political journal. The FBI had political journals. One of the agents stationed in their bureau in Latin America— because in American security the world is split between the CIA which handles international stuff and the FBI which handles domestic stuff but that including all of South and Central America, since South and Central America in the u.s. ruling class mindset is a lesser part of the u.s.a. "It's ours, by imperial birthright", kind of thing. So the FBI is there and they have agents throughout all of the capitals and so forth (as the CIA does, too, obviously). So this FBI agent is writing a theoretical article about how to stop revolution. He's saying something like: "Some people wanted to just stamp it out, get rid of all the revolutionaries. That's impossible because the overwhelming majority of people in the world hate us. They hate American corporations, they hate Wall Street and they're always going to hate us. There's no way to change this."

i'm reading this and i'm, "Hey, you know, they finally got clued in."

He said, so the "We'll just stamp them out like they're insects or something" strategy isn't going to work. Well, actually, you

14

could never get rid of insects. You could tell that in the real world. So, he writes, that's not really practical. It's not a good way strategically to proceed. What we have to do is let everybody hate us. We can't stop that. Let them have anticapitalist, anti-American opinion, fine. But when they organize into groups, when they have dangerous movements, then we don't worry about average people who hate us. That's like confusing the issue. Then we go specifically into those movements, those organizations and we destroy them, as much as possible. There's no talk anywhere in this article of rights, civil liberties, human rights and laws. They don't care about these things. We think they don't care about them and they really don't care about them. Believe me.

A friend was teaching a class of policemen, of cops. The class was report writing, because you think cops are illiterate and everything else and can't sign their names barely, and that was true more than they liked. And so the commanders get these reports back of some major incident and it's completely indecipherable. So you have to give them the usual how-to-write lectures, i guess. Anyway, the thing is, my friend was telling them: gotta learn to write honestly, concisely, clearly, really tell people what happens, when you write that report. So one of the cops jumps to his feet and says, "If I told what I did I'd be in prison!" Everybody applauds, all the other cops applaud. "Right, no more of this accurate report writing shit."

So, this has nothing to do with laws, they don't care about laws. We don't care about them, they don't care about them. We think most people in the world should hate capitalism. They agree, absolutely. You know, that's why they're always trying to mess us up. Otherwise they'd just be laissez faire—"Oh, the revolutionaries, let them do whatever they want, you know, let the protesters run around, you know, give them whatever, it doesn't matter 'cause you know the people will reject them." They don't think that. Believe me, they do not think that.

They think, "We have to really be on top of these people, and sooner is better."

So the Czarist Okhrana had both factions; the "stomp them out" cop faction and the more strategic "we have to manage this" faction. So, they ended up doing things like sponsoring trade unions. Originally, trade unions were illegal, workers want to organize and "Hold it! just a minute! you can't be doing that, damn subversives!" And the Okhrana said to the other cops, "You hold it, you can't stop the workers from doing unions. They are miserable and pissed off and they're absolutely going to do *something*. Why don't we start our own loyal trade unions that are like, you know, hate the boss, demand more money, but love the government. The government is on your side."

So literally the whole legal trade union movement in Russia was started by the political police. If they arrested a band of underground illegal revolutionaries they always would leave one or two people unarrested. They were called breeders. And the reason is really simple. Their worst fear was that rebel movements would start and they wouldn't know anything about it. They wouldn't know anybody in it. That was a really terrible idea to them.

So they'd always leave some people not arrested so when new people came into revolutionary anger and awareness they'd seek out the people who were known as revolutionaries, and since those were under surveillance they would actually just be leading people to be in the files of the secret police. The Okhrana would even sponsor what is now called encapsulated gangs, where there's even like illegal armed terrorist or robbery or guerrilla organizations at the center of which are genuine revolutionaries. But unknown to them mixed in with the new recruits are police agents and they're letting the group proceed because as long as they know everything it's doing, has everything under surveillance, and it has prestige and new people get drawn in, they're just getting an enormous influx of information. The primary thing for political police. And then when they're ready they wipe this group out and set the stage for a next doomed group.

In other words, they want to control dissent, rebellion, manage it. They don't want to try and eliminate it because they don't think that's possible. They want to control it. By controlling the movement as much as they can. There are limits obviously of what anybody can do on this.

To give an example, they were really alarmed about anarchism. Anarchism wasn't strong enough in Russia in the 19th

16

century to overthrow the government, nevertheless it was destabilizing society and more so all the time as most people here know. So they said, well we have to have an antidote. Let's get people to have a different kind of dissenting ideology than this anarchism. So they picked out a variant of socialism, which was popular at the time called Marxism, and they said, well, we'll make this legal. So if you're a dissident and you want to study all these exotic ideas, learn this Marxism. The great Russian encyclopedia said, "We'll even have an entry on Socialism, who could we ask?" The secret police said: "Well, there's a guy named Lenin. You've never heard of him, but he would be a good guy to have write this." So they even wrote to him, like would you please do the entry on socialism for the kind of official Russian encyclopedia?

Clearly they made a few small mistakes in doing it this way, and in fact there's lots of criticism of them in capitalist police theorists circles, like: "The Czar's secret police really messed it up. They were really too arrogant. They thought they could maneuver around everything. Well, see what a mess they made out of it. Blah blah blah."

So, to the security agencies, **the most important thing is not immediate arrests, it's information.** That's the lifeblood of their work. And they're going to infiltrate us to get it. As well as all the other surveillance stuff, okay?

So, when we talk about information, to be honest, we are not primarily talking about what a room of 50 radical people do or don't do because they're actually operating on a much bigger scale. Because don't forget, it's probably true that every single person in this room not only has a file in the computers of the Canadian police, but you certainly have a file in the computers of the u.s. political police. That's like virtually guaranteed.

But its effects run much bigger than that because to them any organization of the oppressed, even "gangs" that they are at the moment de facto sponsoring and manipulating, are potentially really dangerous. They could get out of control, get politically aware. So that in Chicago, the city where i'm from, for example, there are roughly, there are known to be over 100,000 youth in street organizations, i.e. the "gangs", maybe even close to 150,000 something like that. There were as of last year about

73 publicly known street organizations ranging from the Latin Kings to the El Rukns to the Gangster Disciples and so on, the groups of young men who are currently shooting each other like in my neighborhood. The largest of these para-military street organizations have many thousands of members.

Many of these 100,000 plus kids, cause it's a lot, there's a file on. But this isn't necessarily a usual individual police file, or an arrest record. No, often it's a security file. A normal police file might have your name, address, phone number and your arrest and cop contact record. While a security file has all your family, your relations, school and medical record, the places you like to go to drink or recreate, the economic activities you are known to be into, the corners where you hang out, your enemies, the crew in the street organization that you work with, your homies, you know, your fellow soldiers and friends. They have a complete dossier of your activities, on who you are. Of course, being cops, they are also clumsy on the job and get many names and facts wrong as cops do.

It's amazing. They just put enormous resources into that. They brag for example, that like if i were in such a "gang" and i got shot, you know one day, the next day they could go around and prevent the conflict from spreading by simply picking up all the guys in my crew. Because they know who they are. Well, hold it, they're not the ones who shot me, right? So, see, the thing is that the guys in my crew were the guys most likely to be shooting back at the other organization that shot me and so the police would be doing "preventive" arresting, you know to stop the revenge back and forth if they wanted to.

So they're pretty open that they have the intelligence to do this, not that they bother. Which raises a few questions, like so you know each person's crew, their basically criminal work associates, you know, the guys they fight alongside, the fallbacks and where they hang out. And you can just arrest them because somebody in their crew got shot even though they didn't do anything yet? You couldn't even begin to do that unless the state security had updated computer files on the personal lives of masses of oppressed people.

Okay. The thing about security agencies and the political police is that they're not playing cops and robbers. One of

In 2013 the Chicago cops did a big public relations stunt, funded by the National Institute of Justice, that they said would cut down the murder rate. Using a socio-logical computer analysis, they allegedly identified by name the 400 young people most likely to either shoot someone or themselves be shot. A group that as a whole supposedly were 500 times more likely to be involved with violence than mythological "average" Chicagoans. Then area police commanders supposedly visited the homes of persons on the list to warn them to change their lifestyles and associates. How helpful that was (being sarcastic there). The list avoids the predominantly settler North Side, of course, and is only about residents of the heavily New Afrikan and Latino South Side and West Side. What is revealing is the amount of intel-ligence the cops are regularly collecting on the oppressed now.

the big political things, and you're not going to find this in Lenin or something: bour-geois society conditions us to think of rebellion as a cops and robbers game, like their story is it's crime and punish-ment. There's two sides. The state and whatever. They want us to obey the law and we're saying "no", rebelling, we're the criminals breaking the law and that's what rebel-lion is.

Well, that's true in some way and in a deeper way not true. Almost all rebel-lion begins in law-breaking, under capitalism. The prob-lem is that that framework leaves your thinking still within the capitalist system and their values as your reference point.

So that i wish i had a dollar for every time some young guy has told me in a movement meeting or a demonstration, "I'm not afraid to talk to the police because I've done nothing wrong." Well, first of all you're an ass for thinking that. But secondly, it's not about doing something wrong, breaking a law or something, right? Because what's really happening is, it's class war—there's a war between those of us in the oppressed, fighting with the oppressed against capitalism, and those who are defending the system. So this isn't about cops and robbers. But people tend to think of it this way—precisely because that's how bourgeois culture always tries to get us to think of rebellion.

By the way, the "I'm not afraid to talk to the cops because I've done nothing wrong" stuff even on the immediate practical level is not too bright. What the political police want is to update their map. They're mapping the terrain of the rebellions. So if you prove to them, plausibly, that you and your six friends didn't do anything illegal last week—and know nothing about it—that helps them narrow the search for the revs who did. You are just helping complete the map to guide their drone strikes, as it were.

So that, for example, i've talked to guys who are experienced revolutionaries, who've in the past been through armed urban guerrilla groups, who've been in prison, and sometimes they'll say something like, "There's no way the cops could've known anything about us until we got arrested, cause if they'd known a week before, a month before, a year before, well, they would've arrested us then." You see, because this is what my comrade Yaki calls the colonial criminal mentality: that the security cops are about arresting you for violating the law. That's what they care about. That isn't true. They actually don't care about any of that shit. You can't have bigger criminals and law-breakers than the cops.

But people, if you think this way you get completely misled as to what security agencies are doing, **because they will absolutely let you do things to get the deeper information or reposition agents they need to advance their own plans.** We have plans, they have plans. Don't think they're just individual cops enforcing the law, not true and far from it.

The CIA through an agent inside the Brazilian movement learned for example of an airline hijacking in the 1960s about to take place down there. Now you would think that they would stop that right away. No, because to stop that might have exposed their agent. They let the airline hijacking go right on, all kinds of people were terrorized and some killed, and the airline was hijacked but their agent—he'd proven himself as a rev, right? i mean, you can trust him because of actions like the airline hijacking, the whole thing. Anyway, 2 months later he finally found out about the CIA's No.1 target there, a guy named Carlos Marighella, who was one of the main revolutionary guerrilla leaders in Brazil at that time, who wrote the famous "Mini Manual of the Urban Guerrilla", who they absolutely wanted dead. And they finally killed him. So what do they care about a airline hijacking or a bank job or two or ten if they can get somebody they really want, if they get the information they need to put away a whole group or blunt a whole offensive. They absolutely will do these calculated things in cold blood every time.

So this is just practical experience, part of our practical knowledge as revolutionaries. We have to understand these details.

Let me tell you about an FBI penetration of the movement that had mixed results. Of course, the thing about it is that it's completely over and completely documented publicly so we fully know the results and we are not endangering anybody by talking about it.

At the end of the '60s, i was recruited... i was living on the Southside of Chicago and was recruited by a small group of working-class women to join a community, a revolutionary community group far on the other side of the city. And i got talked into it, so moved to join this organization. It was a working-class, mostly white revolutionary group.

So, this group had an interesting history. When Students for a Democratic Society (or SDS), the nationwide white university radical whatever mass anti-war people of that time went on the offensive, one of the things they wanted to do was to break out of their class world. They started student-run organizing projects in poor working class neighborhoods, often using the name "Jobs Or Income Now" or JOIN. Newark, Baltimore, Chicago, a few other places. So in Chicago these student radicals "colonized" one particular poor neighborhood, temporarily moved activists in there to live, and started organizing. One result was a small street organization of Southern white youth that was political. First organized to do a protest march on the local cop station, against police harassment of poor white youth. And the middle-class university radicals were overjoyed. The working class Southern whites who were supposed to be so racist and patriotic redneck and against the movement, well, they had convinced some of them in this neighborhood to join the movement. To be anti-war and for the Black revolutionaries and even ally with them and so on.

To some degree, though, those middle-class radicals were way inexperienced and didn't quite know what they were doing. When i got into that scene, it was surprising politically. The street organization, which had a hard core of a couple of dozen members mostly from teenagers to guys in their mid-twenties, and maybe a supporters layer of that many, had a small group of about five or six guys who were central, who were leaders in a somewhat informal way. Everyone looked to them to start things, but two of these guys were clearly like fascists. You have to keep in mind whenever you go down, all the way down into the oppressed and very poor, there isn't one class there but always two. The lower working class and the lumpen do not just coexist, they share the same streets and homes and families, they're people mixed in with each other fighting to survive on the same shared terrain together.

One guy in particular seemed an obvious fascist and an obvious danger, because he really did want to lead things his way. Tom had grown up in the neighborhood, where his mom was still a "working woman" in the same slum residence hotel they had lived in since he was a kid. He had grown up with many of the other guys, and they all knew him as one of the smartest guys around. Actually, he had even gone to Stanford on a scholarship (few of the other poor white guys had even gone to secondary school). But Tom had dropped out, had kicked around at a different job, and finally come back home to join the movement. And he was pushing definite strong politics, which to me tripped all the alarm bells.

Say what you want about him, Tom did have game. In 1969 the Panthers had called for their United Front Against Fascism, a national conference to unite the left against fascism in America under their leadership. Whether that's a good or bad idea, not germane to us here. The main Maoist group in America at that time, called the Progressive Labor Party, said, like, "This is outrageous, this is a fraud. The Panthers, who are they? They don't follow Chairman Mao, they have the little red book, but the only true Maoist leadership here is us. So therefore we're going to go to the conference, but we're going to stay a block away. We'll form a line in the street around the conference." What we had heard from the movement grapevine, was that they were threatening to physically stop anybody that came to support the Panthers. Sounded like they'd lost it mentally, going to just beat the shit out of anyone and basically prevent them from going to the conference. Don't know.

But that was a mental moment made in heaven for manipulators like Tom. It isn't true that someone else's bad politics like that early Maoist group trying to play little stalin, only effects them and doesn't hurt us. So he quickly organized a group of our guys from the neighborhood, this was while he was still in the group. They flew out there and they just literally marched right at the Progressive Labor guys who were led by—they actually had their martial arts class there with an instructor with a black belt—Tom went right at the PL karate instructor and punched the shit right out of him. Frankly, because Tom had been seriously fighting people and hurting people his whole life, so you might have got yourself a black belt in a dojo somewhere but this isn't the same deal as getting mixed up in a chaotic street brawl.

So that Summer we heard him saying, pretty smoothly, "Hey, all these black people, they're talking about black power. I'm all for that. That's wonderful. I love them so much we should adopt the same slogan for us—White Power! That should be our slogan, White Power." So some of the guys were influenced, like, "Oh, that sounds pretty cool, white power, I like that." What Tom wasn't telling them was that "White Power" was right then an official slogan of the neo-nazi movement in the u.s. And had the added treacherous appeal of seeming to be only "equal" with Black Power, while denying that in "race" terms settlers didn't need to demand power since they already had it all.

We were saying, "Hold it, just a minute, we might want to think about that, you know, whoa, whoa, whoa." And so Tom went around everybody else, convinced a couple guys to go with him and they went to the button shop and they got a thousand buttons printed up saying, "White people gotta get it on." What exactly does that mean anyway, right? But there's kind of a common theme in the work he was doing, you know. It's all about white people being angry and doing things by themselves and for themselves and that's the main thing. There's kind of a pattern about what he was doing.

Anyway so the women—mostly it was a small group of women—you see all the propaganda about this group done in the left talked about guys. How they were like a street gang of pro-movement white guys. Teens and men who had come over to the revolution, wonderful, but it was odd that it was almost like there were no women there. But it turns out that there really were women there, and they thought this was really a bad scene. Their guys are really getting turned around.

So first of all they went and recruited some of us to come in, though we didn't know what the hell was going on. And—the other thing was by the way this neighborhood was not all set-tler. For example it was overwhelmingly poor but it was not all white. It was the major neighborhood center for Native people in the Chicago area, for example. In a similar way, it was a center for some of the Asian peoples. There were 15,000 indigenous people in the neighborhood (and over 6,000 Asians), which wasn't really mentioned in the left propaganda or anything because of the importance of the whiteness to the left of the young guys they were organizing...

So the women with the group started recruiting a few people of color and women with civil rights movement experience, basically just to make certain there wasn't a racist outbreak going on there. And then they convinced some guys, they talked to some of the guys and said "look, we have to deal with this, what's going on". Two of the women in particular i remem-ber—one was an older woman, they were both older from my point of view, could have been in their 40s or 50s. One of the women was Native, and disabled and had 2 kids and was on welfare, and the other woman who was truly leading this was a white southern woman from Appalachia who had no educa-tion at all except that she had been through union organizing battles as a poor woman working in a factory, and had the klan try to shoot at them and had been communist baited in her town and whatnot for being against racism and so she actually had experienced politics.

So i came to this meeting and the women said you don't know what's happening, just vote with us, don't worry. i said "okay" and they called out one of these guys, the guy who was Tom, the white power dude who was causing all the trouble.

The thing was... Tom was, the guys knew he was a trouble-maker, they said that's just how he is 'cause they grew up with him in the neighborhood. He grew up on the streets with them. They all knew each other for years. So to say, Tom is no good and to kick him out, the guys couldn't do this.

But the women they were serious, they just said, "Tom we have to talk about you. The fact is you're always causing trouble, and second, you're a damn racist. No matter what you say, you're a racist. And third, when we add that up, we think you're an agent. Why else would you be doing this shit, right? Except that you gotta be an agent. So, we're taking a vote. Our motion is: Your ass gets kicked out. Oh, by the way, you and all the university students. Part of our motion is that you have to be a worker, a working class person, to be in the group, like it's a union now. All the university students who are being famous at our expense, we thank you for all you've done for us, we love you, and you can now leave because we're now voting to kick you out, too." There were some surprised people in that room.

And bingo! Tom was doing his usual excuses, "oh, it's politics that's so hard for me to learn, 'cause I had no education". Though he had no trouble getting into Stanford. He was hanging his head and whining, "I wanna learn, I'm sorry, give me another chance." But the women weren't going to stand for that shit. The women said, "No, Tom. We've known you your whole life and you're a racist and now you're a damn agent, get out of the room." So they kicked him out.

So Tom went and we thought, oh, that's the end of that. The guy's been kicked out of his own community group by people who've known him his whole damn life. Hey, he's gone permanently, we don't have to worry about him, good or bad, whatever he is. Yeah, we were wrong about that!

Well, Tom went to the university student movement leaders, and they were nationally important people on the left at that point and they'd been kicked out of the neighborhood and were pissed. Tom played them, using his men's solidarity angle. It must have been something like, "Yeah, those bitches, they kicked us out, well I'm with you bro'" and ka-ching! The next movement radical conference, there's Tom being vouched for by these middle-class student leaders. Damn, we know he's an agent, but suddenly he's back in the movement again!

He goes back to California, to Stanford, not to school but to hang out, he makes his living doing armed robberies and boasting about it. He's knocking over a liquor store, a grocery store, whatever, he's doing armed robberies, selling drugs, stealing drugs at gunpoint to sell, never gets arrested, gee, wonder why. And beating people up. He's picking fights in the movement. You know, he'll come to a meeting and, "I don't like what you're saying", suddenly he will lunge himself across the room. He was actually really good at fighting. And he'll start pounding the crap outta some guy.

So, half the people in the movement said, "Wow, what a revolutionary! Poor, working class, so angry he can't contain himself, he's gotta be a revolutionary." The other half of the people in the room in the movement said, "You know, he's a stone mental case, he's so crazy that the FBI would never have somebody like that. He's totally undisciplined and untrustworthy. So, he may be bad news, but he's not an agent." So both sides, for different reasons agreed that he wasn't an agent.

Only problem: Tom *was* an agent. Tom was crazy like a fox. Tom was just a fascist, that's all. So, eventually through the movement he got introduced to the Black Panther Party in Northern Cal and Tom reminded them of a very—to him—important moment in history and this is again where we see the relationship between bad politics and bad security in a practical sense.

Back at that conference, remember, Tom and the guys completely mopped the streets with the Progress Labor activists and sent the Maoists leaving, running for their lives. So Tom could later remind the Panther leadership, "Remember that? I was the guy who did that and I know all this stuff—martial arts, bomb making, I can teach marksmanship, I was in the marines, I was in intelligence in the marines. I was really good at, you know, interrogating people, wink wink (i.e torturing people). You got agents, bro', in your group, I can help you with this."

So the Panthers say, wow! They're impressed: a settler guy who had fought on the streets to defend us and he's got all these skills and now he's gonna help us find the agents. So Tom launched on a spree of bad jacketing honest ordinary people in the Panthers, "Yeah that guy, he looks like an agent, beat the crap out of him until he talks, throw him out", torturing people, the whole thing.

It culminated, he had gotten a ranch up in the mountains he called "Guevara Ranch" where he had bomb making classes, literally. So one night they lured a leading Black Panther revolutionary activist named Fred Bennett to "Guevera Ranch". Fred Bennett was leading the defense around getting support for George Jackson and the other Soledad brothers in prison, the black revolutionaries who were leading the struggle in prisons in California at that time. He was the chairman of that committee. Anyway he was killed. He was tortured and shot to death and his body was set on fire, burned and buried, etc. So nobody knew what happened. All of a sudden a couple weeks later the FBI and the police descend, they dig up the body, they started raiding Panther offices and they get a witness saying so-and-so and so-and-so was involved.

Tom suddenly appears in suit and tie before the u.s. senate subcommittee on intelligence to explain how, "Yes, it's terrible the Panthers, they're killing their own people, they're so demented and violent that they're torturing and killing other Panthers. Terrible." Actually of course Tom instigated the whole thing and he was proud as shit of it. For a settler fascist, to have manipulated the vaunted Black Panther Party into killing one of its own best people—and have done it with the stupid help of those "rich university leftists" that he hated so much— he really loved that.

Okay, when you reel that back what do you see?

What you see is a young undeveloped left in which a small group of working-class women figured out who an agent was, and how dangerous he was. Because more than just being smart, Tom was a very aggressive and manipulative guy. And they thought they had gotten rid of him, just banished him out of the movement. But some middle-class guys who had gone to NYUs and Berkeleys, those young white guys said in effect, "Who cares what those women think!" They were sure they knew better.

Tom the "revolutionary", they passed him onto the Panthers who absolutely should have known better, except of course they were caught up in their own patriarchal thinking—revolutionary attitude that's male attitude, aggression, being more violent, forcing your will on people, being the tough important guy... Tom looked great to them!

Well, a lot of people actually ended up getting hurt out of it. They only surfaced one killing because the feds couldn't admit that they had their agent do a torturing and killing spree through the movement. Tom was like, "I was nowhere near anything and I never knew what happened. I just heard about it later when I couldn't do anything except tell the FBI, blah, blah, blah." Complete lies, the grapevine said.

So here's this mini tragedy. Certainly a successful disrupting of movement activity, that should have been stopped at any number of points, but **bad politics covered for agents. So we don't need good politics because that makes us into super people because it doesn't. It's that bad politics—like opportunism, patriarchy, sexism, class privilege—rips up the fabric of our terrain, the area of our radical culture and it weaves instead into that terrain all their old oppressor politics, their values.** At which point we're confused, it's all backwards. We're alice-in-wonderland now on their side, their ground, so to speak, even though we don't have their views.

So i'm just going to stop here.

The Politics of Security

a presentation by J. Sakai

Monday, May 27th, 6:30 pm

@ QPIRG Concordia
1500 deMaisonneuve W., rm. 204
(metro Guy-Concordia)

Wheelchair accessible

Whisper translation into French
Traduction chuchoté vers le français

Got questions? info@kersplebedeb.com

QUESTIONS & ANSWERS

Moderator: So if anyone has any questions?

Q: When you said that the American police had a security file on everyone in this room, I was wondering what you were basing that on. I was wondering if it would apply to people just in this room or if it would apply to people outside on the street.

A: Well, i don't know how many people on the street they have investigative files on, but i'm pretty certain that if you're a Canadian revolutionary or a radical in any real way, other than reading a magazine once a year, they're definitely going to be interested in you. They're absolutely into accumulating as much personal information as they can. It makes their job easier. That's just the long and short of it, and they're paid for it, so it's a major activity of theirs. Remember, to Washington some young activists in Canada equals "international terrorists", a non-u.s. citizen category in which anything goes, there are no rules or limitations on what they can do.

And these are questions that never get asked enough, among ourselves, about what it means. **And the reason we need to push the whole underlying question of politics is because a lot of people particularly guys try to present security as an area essentially where it's about cool techniques or it's technology. That's completely not what it's about.** And in terms of bad politics of every kind on this, there's a lot of it around.

For example... i actually brought with me... this is a curiosity piece from the past that i plucked from my bookshelf. This is the Communist Party Manual on Organization printed here first in the 1930s by the u.s. communist party which by that time had 200,000 members or something, controlled entire industrial unions, had strong arm squads to deal with people who bothered them and in fact, although it's not publicly admitted, sometimes had assassination units to deal with special comrades who they considered traitors. So this was like a real deal, this was not six guys alone in a room. But although it comes from 1930s, it got reprinted and distributed all over again in 1975 to help guide that new generation of Marxist-Leninists rebuild in the u.s. It keeps getting recycled all over again.

So they had a whole chapter on how they should safeguard the party against informers and spies. And it says:

"Agent provocateurs are planted in the party either by the police department, Department of Justice, patriotic organizations or counterrevolutionary Trotskyites disrupting the work of the party. The methods they use are: A) Creating sentiment against the leadership of the party B) Systematic disruptive criticism against the line of the party."

This goes on and on. This is like clearly total bullshit, right? On all these different levels. Clearly, this has nothing to do with security. They want to browbeat everybody into following their orders from the central committee or whoever. And if you're not following their orders then maybe you're a spy or agent, and that kind of arm-twisting bullshit.

So you think, hopefully you think, well this is kind of stupid. You think this was way back in the 1930s. It's gone forever in our modern age. Well it isn't. **Sometimes people still use**

"security" as a club against people they disagree with or don't like in the movement. An ultra bad idea. To be specific, an ultra bad *opportunist* idea. Many activists think opportunism is only about someone selling out for a good job or some cash courtesy of the ruling class, and we do see that. But more commonly we get hit with another kind of opportunism, that's people—sometimes even with what they believe are good motives—putting factional interests, the little interest of their group or tendency or their own political interests ahead of the needs and health of the struggle as a whole.

Like about a year ago or something, somebody pointed out to me that there was a letter in "Anarchy" magazine which said that a certain anarchist, whom we know as a real pain in the ass personally, was not born in the u.s. The guy was an immigrant and therefore under the actual letter of the u.s. laws, being a publicly identified anarchist, the FBI could deport him. So the letter-writer went on, given that he is really well known, doesn't the fact that they're *not* deporting him mean that he should be considered an agent by us?

i read this letter and i thought, "This is completely full of it". So we're supposed to let the FBI decide by their actions who we label as an agent or not? You know, by what the other side does? If they don't arrest you or something then that somehow "proves" you're an agent?! This is like crack addict thinking, frankly. Why did they even print that malicious letter?

Anybody who's done any security work knows that if you said to someone who really is an agent, "We are going to kick you out of the movement unless you agree to follow the line of whoever, you know follow the line of Noam Chomsky or Joseph Stalin or whatever". This guy's an agent, most of the time he doesn't care about left ideas! He's going to say, "Oh yeah, i agree with whatever leadership 150%. i'll agree to any dumb idea you have since i don't care about your movement anyway!"

What does he care? He'll agree to any idea you have. There's no amount of brown nosing or yessing an agent will do to get inside, if that's what his job is. As opposed, say, to causing fights and personal disputes and throwing sand in the wheels. So the Communist Party that printed that bullshit, 20 years later was being completely crushed by McCarthyism during the 1950s Cold War. Historians now estimate that 1 out of every 3 of their members was a police agent by that time. Well, good job on security, you guys!

You know, it turns out that following the leadership blindly, agreeing to everything, no matter what, it's not a good idea from anybody's point of view. The more critical, the more open, the more many-sided our dialogue and our thinking is and our examination of politics is, the more agents tend to stand out because they're not of us in that sense.

Q: You were mentioning how Czarist police had this division and more political policing has this division between "line them up and shoot them all" and something much more nuanced. I don't know if you have heard of Frank Kitson? The Brigadier General, the British General, he wrote the manual on counterinsurgency based on Malaysia and Northern Ireland. I've taken it based on what i've read as the default basis that anglo-american policing is based on.

He talks about three stages, which combines both. So the first stage is when movements just exist, and what they should do is just find out everything about them, which reinforces what you were saying about how they want to have all the information.

The second stage is when those movements become more disruptive and the third is when they become revolutionary. The point is: When they become revolutionary you have all the names, you know who to kill. But in the meantime you should be more subtle about it.

In Quebec for example, the second stage was during the October Crisis, when they had all these names of people to arrest, or who they thought they should arrest. The 3rd stage was seen in Chile in the Pinochet Coup or after the Suharto Coup when they literally killed hundreds and thousands and millions of people, so I'm wondering whether we should posit these things as opposites or whether they can actually coexist, knowingly coexist as political policing.

Reading this 3 months later, i mostly remember how exhausted i was by that point in the discussion, and how it was hard for me to even keep in mind what the point was never mind being coherent. Our comrade was insightful bringing Gen. Frank Kitson and his counter-insurgency work up, because people speculate that he represents the most sophisticated repressive strategy in use. Certainly he's a real "name" in the field. Several other comrades at the meeting also informally asked us to discuss Kitson, which i completely didn't do. So here's finishing this up better.

To start, there's several questions wrapped around each other here. One is whether the classic tension has been overcome between the "let's just round 'em up, shoot them & imprison them" school of policing versus the more strategic police approach of manipulating and trying to permanently manage dissent? Have the two been blended by innovations like Kitson's counter-insurgency plan into one smoothly integrated club?

The quick answer is no. One big reason that the old-school tendency of simply attacking dissent with raw often illegal state violence never dies is simple: that's what many police and military innately want to do, what they love doing! Same with the ruling class.This is their subculture, their default setting, which they revert to at every opportunity. These opposing state security tendencies may appear in public relations as a harmonious strategy, but in reality are always in inner conflict pushing to dominate one over the other.

This is the real world not the theory world. Like, in my neighborhood last holidays, between xmas and New Years, the police did a coordinated series of over 20 drug raids to remind all the Mexican emigrants and poor New Afrikan families that santa claus was a white man with a club ruling them. "Happy New Year!" First we heard the rapid footsteps of big guys racing upstairs. Then the ritual shout of "Police! Open up!" followed a second later by a big smash as they broke into the next door apartment. It was the "B team". Not the SWAT dudes with all black combat garb, military helmets and assault rifles. But the "tactical intervention" squad, a half-dozen tall, young white boys in dark blue "tac" police coveralls and shotguns and pistols. Then we heard the "thud" after "thud" as they charged inside and knocked down to the floor and cuffed everyone in the apartment. This all took only seconds. All i could think of that moment, was to admire how disciplined their little daughter was, how she didn't cry or scream even though she must have been terrified.

Then an hour of capitalist fun overturning and smashing open all the furniture and cabinets searching for something illegal. Finally, after not finding anything except the big illegal thing—poverty—the euro-settler "tac" team uncuffed the undocumented Mexican family and just left like Batman, running downstairs for their squad cars laughing and shouting at each other happily, still on an adrenaline high. Give this everyday violence up, you got to be kidding? They live for this shit.

During the 1980s, some left writers in the u.s. began pointing to Kitson as a source of important warnings. This was mostly because small groups there & then such as the Revolutionary Armed Task Force and the black liberation army-coordinating committee were pursuing urban guerrilla activity in a still undeveloped way. Comrades needed to see what world-class capitalist anti-guerrilla strategy and tactics looked like. In particular, Kitson's heavy reliance on the tactic of pseudo-gangs or countergangs rang warning bells in our minds back then. To best check out that earlier discussion, you can read the paper "Pseudo-Gangs" in the June 1983 issue of the anonymous left journal "S1" on the kersplebedeb website.

But, no, Gen. Kitson's writings don't represent the latest shape of modern political policing. He rose up through the commissioned ranks through three British imperial counter-insurgency campaigns of the 1950-60s—in Kenya, Malaya and Northern Ireland. His campaigns are important as part of capitalist warfare in the era of the old Western colonial empires. But they have been superceded by newer strategy in this neo-colonial world.

It is true that he helped draw the tactic of pseudo-gangs or counter-gangs out of the bloody closet of Britain's Special Branch cops, who had used it way way back in the Palestine colony days against both Arab and Jewish underground organizations (not that it did them much good). That is, Kitson was relying on a specific political police tool that went back all the way to the founding fathers, i.e. the Czarist Okhrana who had used it. But like today's CIA drone warfare this was and is only a tactic used in specific situations not an overall strategy.

A pseudo-gang or counter-gang, incidentally, is when the political police form an imitation underground revolutionary cell or band; usually using some former guerrillas or rebels they have captured and convinced to "flip"and work for them. In order to infiltrate and often not simply to do arrests but to misdirect the whole insurgency. This goes beyond getting a few more comrades arrested. This type of tactic particularly extended into public mass movements, can have strategic impact. Even stalling and then derailing struggles. For instance, when particularly counter-productive left cults get artificially energized with hard-working agents and a tankful of government cash. They can appear to be a very successful "vanguard" that absorbs more and more new activists into a political crash and burn.

Gen. Kitson neither developed nor led the counter-gangs that he became so famous for after "Mau Mau" in the 1950s; that was all done quietly by the British empire's police Special Branch. But Kitson saw the opportunity to grab all the public credit and get famous for work the army didn't even do. Incidentally, the Special Branch officer who developed and personally commanded the countergangs in Kenya was expelled in the 1960s after Kenyan Independence, of course; he ended up spending 20 profitable years running the feared secret police for the royal family of Bahrain.

Also, remember what the most basic thing is we learned about capitalism's "experts" on repression? That they are always lying to us. Like, just a few years ago, the public was told how u.s. Gen. Petraeus had supposedly brilliantly led the American occupation to victory in Iraq over the "terrorists", right? Mostly b.s. in reality. Kitson is just the previous NATO generation's "Petraeus". What Kitson did is nothing like what he claimed in print.

Gen. Kitson's work was part of the warfare of the previous colonial era of the 1930s-1950s, and is not directly transferable to today's more complex neo-colonial period (what capitalism calls "Globalization" and academics call "neo-liberalism"). His writings are part of modern total warfare in and against the colonial periphery, not so much policing inside the imperialist metropolis. Although Kitson himself didn't agree, of course. In his once-classified paper for the Imperial General Staff, Low-Intensity Operations, Kitson rashly outlined how their army units should be spread out to be a secret part of all British local governing down to the village level, using pseudo-gangs to crush things like trade union strikes, ethnic minority protest campaigns and other social "problems". He even rashly revealed that pseudo-gangs were then being used in the u.s. empire against New Afrikan militants. That was all supposed to be secret. The resulting leaks and liberal scandal and public outrage put the ever-ambitious Gen. Kitson back in his cushy place.

Kitson's abstract pronouncements about neat stages of intelligence-gathering and deployment of dead white men's tricks like pseudo-gangs, are nothing like his own dirty military reality. **Intelligence-gathering doesn't quietly precede repression as its own stage of well-behaved activity, rather it itself is the product of constant intervention and repression in peoples' lives.** In order for his beloved pseudo-gangs to work in Kenya (the first and only war where they became the primary combat tactic), two much larger weapons had to be rumbled out of the garage and put into play.

That was what in today's CIA terminology were "population regroupment" and "enhanced interrogation" programs. Out of the 1.5 million Kikuyus alive in Kenya then, fully 1 million were uprooted from their traditional villages at riflepoint and forced to move into new locations chosen for them, into improvised guarded settlements. Where their movements were restricted and their access to food kept at starvation levels so that no supplying of the rural guerrillas could take place. Massive interrogation activities went on constantly, particularly of the over 77,000 Kikuyu arrested or captured as "Mau Mau" and held separately in prison camps at their height. These British interrogations were based on mass executions as coercion and mass torturing and mutilations such as castration. Rape was such an ordinary activity that it wasn't even thought of as part of torture, but rather as a "perk" that the "civilized" British had granted their Afrikan mercenary troops and themselves to do at will.

Robbing families of their scant money and possessions, extortion, torturing to death, killing to settle personal scores and spontaneous killing for the enjoyment of it, were common British military activities against the unarmed civilian population. It reached scandalous proportions even by European colonial standards (which is a statement by itself), and Kenya's British police commissioner Arthur Young resigned rather than be further implicated. In 2013, after a long grassroots campaign that went mostly unreported here, some 1500 Kikuyu torture interrogation survivors received official letters of apology from the Crown, as well as promises of small cash reparations. But most of the many thousands of torture victims were long dead. Officially the British Empire claimed 11,000 "Mau Mau" deaths by their forces in the 1952-1956 "Emergency", but actually the daily killing was so widespread and constant that no real body count was kept. Figures in the many tens of thousands are heard.

Now, can you imagine the capitalist state being able to get away with or even desiring such a disruptive bloodbath in Manhattan's Upper West Side or at Montreal's Concordia University? If what happens here was proportionate to what Kitson & Co. did in the Kikuyu uprising, we would be talking *about forcibly moving millions of euro-settlers to tent cities in barren areas, behind barbed wire and under armed guards, torturing hundreds of thousands of young white women and men in an uncontrollable bloodbath. Even done on a much lesser scale it would be a big systemic shock. That's what Kitson's actual strategy would mean if applied to the privileged metropolitan population of empire and its often spirited but frustrated left.*

To say that this would be hugely counter-productive as a way of coping with the actually existing left here is a big understatement. Which is why the more experienced and practical levels of state power gently spanked Gen. Kitson and reminded him to follow orders and confine his insane homicidal schemes to indigenous and neo-colonial societies, to the Bantustan, to the ghetto and the rez and the barrio. Not to dream of putting settler anti-nuke committees into concentration camps or gleefully maiming white trade union dissenters. Unnecessary overkill and rocking their whole boat were out, to say the least.

Q. continued: And the other one was about bad politics. So bad politics is sexist, macho behavior, but it strikes me that in 2013, the political police know that and practice feminist anti-oppressive kinds of behaviour. In a really superficial way that movie "Zero Dark Thirty" which is highlighting female CIA agents who were essentially responsible for finding out where Bin Laden was, using techniques that were more using the mind rather than macho torture or what have you. There are examples of infiltration where it is not the Brandon Darby type macho person but rather a more subtle, listening and nurturing type person who gets a lot of information by being a good stereotypical feminist or what have you. So i'm wondering whether we have to modify our idea of what bad politics is because political police knows that well enough and knows that that macho person will be more targeted.

My 3rd point is: I find that the fear of the police knowing everything debilitates people from being active and the statement that you made that every revolutionary has a file on them—is there more of a nuance to that? In terms of if you're politically active, if you're publicly active, if you've done certain things maybe? It strikes me as sometimes the fear of what the state can do debilitates people from being active rather than what they're actually doing and certainly there's plenty examples of infiltration and stories we can share of their overwhelming power, but there are also examples of people being able to overcome that despite their resources.

Those are 3 really big things I wanted to get it all out and have you respond to.

J: Well, the thing about security, i agree about a lot of things you say. In terms of them learning to be more nuanced, absolutely. Though, you know, a lot of times they use a range of agents, approach wise, as well as short-term and long-term infiltrations with different characteristics, always have. But this is a funny world about fear...

This isn't a defensive battle is the main thing. When we conceive of security as an area of struggle, that doesn't mean what security is, police are trying to harass us, arrest us, whatever infiltrate our organizations and we have to defend ourselves. This is not what it's about. We're struggling against capitalism in this area. **We're on the offense as much as we can, not defense.** Yes, they're going to have files on lots of people, they'll photograph us, etc. But we're fighting, and that's even in the small sense. Pick your battles but people are fighting. They always have.

For example, it used to be a custom that a lot of people in the movement didn't get their picture taken. Family photo? include me out! You go to their house, no pictures of them, no photos of them at all. They were laughed at, "Oh man, you're just out of it! The cops have ten thousand pictures of you at demonstrations so why do you have to worry about that?"

That's true, but the thing is, **they like us have lots of room to mess up in daily life, in the daily details of work. We want to give them every opportunity on every practical detail to do it wrong,** and we want to work it that way. So for example when Assata Shakur popped in New Jersey—so suddenly she's not buried in prison but a fugitive, suddenly she's gone, wanted posters go up all over the country put up by the FBI. One problem: the photo they used of Assata was a surveillance photo from what i could tell, and you actually would never recognize Assata meeting her on the street from that

A few years ago a comrade was telling me about an "outrage" that happened to him at a protest march. He had taken his young child, carrying the kid finally at the head of the march, and suddenly some black bloc or someone behind them he couldn't see started throwing stones and bottles at the cops. The cops charged them with clubs, of course, and he was really scared that his kid would get hurt. And really pissed at the "anarchists", not that he knew who had started shit irresponsibly he thought—he angrily called them "agents provocateurs" even. My own take: what's that old left saying, "A revolution is not a tea party, or writing an essay, or painting a picture, or doing embroidery; it cannot be so refined ..."? Many children have been hurt in the struggle. Times i took my kids when they were little on a demo, and was worried for them. Don't take your kid to a demo if you want them to be completely safe. And if you want the movement to do completely guaranteed safe actions, sign up in a different world not this real one.

photograph. Funny thing happened: a group was putting out one of those support Assata posters, with a accurate picture of her face on it. And rads had to go tell them, "Hey, good work but you should blur her picture up some, make her less recognizable." It never occurred to the comrades that the FBI had missed the ball completely and we didn't want to accidentally do some of their job for them.

So why did they do it? Why did they use a non-functional wanted picture? Who knows. But i want to give them every chance to do it. That's not a stray thought, but a basic principle of our work.You better believe i'm not mailing photos to the FBI, because they can mess it up too.

Marilyn Buck, the settler anti-imperialist urban guerrilla, exact same thing with her. She became a fugitive, escaped from prison, etc. They put out a government wanted poster. Photograph from what i could tell came from an old college newspaper, kind of like a junky social news article or something. Absolutely would not recognize her after many years in prison and the struggle from that photograph.

Their use of these things this is part of their political work. They're not doing it just to arrest us, they're doing it to criminalize us, to create fear, to picture us as the evil people, to get the people to be afraid, shouldn't be near them, etc. And we fight them on this.

There was a young artist who took part in a militant demonstration against the previous settler colonial government of South Africa (before it went neo-colonial) which sent its Springboks sports team, famous team, to tour America and build support for their regime, their colonialist racial dictatorship. There was a very militant and small demonstration when they were at the JFK airport in New York against them in the course of which one of cops protecting them was injured. They arrested a young woman artist and said she did it. i don't know whether she did, i wasn't there, i don't know what happened. But she didn't like her chances, 'cause they were talking like about 20 years. She didn't like her chances going to court, so she got bailed out, she disappeared, and hasn't been seen since in public here, never was caught.

So they issued a special wanted poster. It wasn't your normal wanted poster. It went up in the subways. It was a long strip of 5 wanted felons' mug shots. There's her, the young woman artist in the middle, and there's 2 guys on each side of the strip: on each side there's one rapist and one murderer. A rapist and a murderer and then her. That's who she is supposed to be like. They don't think they're going to catch her that way. No, it's their whole part of criminalizing us, right? Like, they're saying "This wasn't a political struggle, it's these vicious, criminal, violent people."

So there's this wave of spontaneous anger from the women's community in New York (she was a lesbian), from anti-war people who supported the struggle against apartheid in South Africa. People just saying, "I have a couple of hours this evening I'm going to the subway". People just walking the trains car to car ripping down these damn wanted posters. Within a week there weren't any, basically, people couldn't find any. And the pigs figured out that, "Oh, we better not put them up because when we put them up, they'll just rip them down."

So they try to maneuver, this has nothing to do with crime stuff, it's a political thing. They try to maneuver against us and we answered them spontaneously and basically wiped their gambit out. Well, that's part of security, it's part of how we should think about things.

Once we were in a struggle where security and guarding ourselves against FBI attack kept merging into the larger struggle against the system, in a way we couldn't forget. We were based in a New Afrikan poor community, a "black" neighborhood and the FBI was concerned about it and they didn't like the struggle which was revolutionary and against the system, against the government and stuff. And so they started a political campaign which had 2 stages. They figured out the 1st thing to do was to criminalize the activity politically so they picked out this one young white woman—and this shows that they know things—and she was important because there were two main elements in the struggle. There were the young street guys and women who were teenagers or young 20s who were the tactical force, and there were the older women who were the strategic leadership mostly like mothers and grandmothers. And that one woman activist was one of the various links between the two elements, because she was running with both groupings. However it came about, that's just how it worked. Their intelligence figured that out.

So one day we wake up and her photo is on the front page of every daily newspaper in the city. "Communist Agent Trained in Cuba in Infiltration Techniques Found in Negro Community Misleading those Poor Innocent People Into Rebelling" type shit, it was that crude. As if this young woman could ever create a mass rebellion in a New Afrikan neighborhood, right?

Then their next step was they were going to raid the block that she was staying in, squatting in that neighborhood, they were going to have a big raid. They could've just sent two guys in, made an appointment and arrested her, but that's not what they wanted. They wanted to make a big show of force, right, that "we're in charge", that they have the power and they were going to arrest her in front of everybody; they literally brought in like dozens of agents and cops, to search the whole block and seize people and do all this shit.

Now the night before this guy who was like "Silky"—he would dress like a pimp but he was actually a full-time police informant, he was actually a major "black" informer on the South Side of Chicago at the time and everybody knew that and he didn't hide it. And so he's also armed and a really dangerous guy, he wouldn't have been alive otherwise. He came up to some of us in a bar and he said, "They're going to do this raid tomorrow morning at 8 o'clock, they're going to come get so and so, so you should tell her, just spread the word" and he left.

So that night we talked to the mothers and grandmothers who were the leaders and said, "You're going to get raided by the cops tomorrow, that's what so and so said." One of the women got angry and said, "There's nothing that the white cops can find that we don't want them to find". So our young woman was going to leave the block, so she'd get arrested at some other point somewhere else, not in their neighborhood, but the women said, "No, you stay right here honey."

And the cops and the FBI descended on the whole block and are banging on doors and there's a crowd of young kids suddenly who were entranced by them. So they'd go in and there would 4 or 5 cops and there would be kids, little kids in the way, who were yelling and laughing and throwing balls and saying play with me. What are they gonna do? They can't shoot this little kid. On the other hand they can't be doing anything because they're dragging this little kid. And everyone is in the way. Meanwhile this woman was being moved...where the cops weren't, right? ... At one point this young woman was hidden for a long time all the way up on a building roof, guided by a young New Afrikan lesbian (our girl later said that it was nice, with a furious FBI raid going on below them as the two were enjoying the great view of the neighborhood and comparing notes on Chicago's main lesbian bar, which they both had tried out).

After about 6 hours the state finally gave up. The whole damn block united against them and they couldn't do a bloody thing.

So they had attempted to make it their terrain, the security police, it was going to be their terrain. They were going to terrorize everybody. They were going to show that nobody could defy them, that they ruled it. But it became the oppressed peoples' terrain, particularly the women and children's terrain, because they turned out to be the winners.

So when i'm talking about security i'm not talking about simply defending ourselves. It's not that. It's the constant struggle with their security agencies—just another area—with capitalism.

Q: I was wondering, you pointed out before, there's no "Security for Dummies" book where you can learn various techniques and various strategies but that seems like that's something that's widely deficient within our movement and people are getting infiltrated quite easily by police surveillance. As you were pointing out, it's the tradition that that information get handed down orally, but if we don't have that information how would you recommend that we cultivate a stronger sense of security within our movements?

J: i can't say that i know the answers. i don't. Like for example the NATO 5 in Chicago, who were set up to be guilty of trying to throw Molotov cocktails at Mayor Emmanuel's house. Popular idea, of course. But you shouldn't let the police agent set you up to do it, right? In every mobilization, in every organization, people have to quietly organize themselves to take responsibility for teaching and training.

So, you start to learn things and when there are problems like with radical environmental actions or the NATO 5, well ... The problem wasn't with these guys who were perhaps injudicious in how they related to this cop, it's the fact that if we don't assume responsibility for politics this is the result. People come, who are not educated, they're let's say naïve, they're vulnerable to being worked up by the cops, let's say. This is one problem. It's not the biggest problem, necessarily. There's nobody looking out after them. There's nobody saying, "If you want to be doing controversial stuff, don't be doing it with people you didn't know before yesterday. And you have no idea who this guy is. You know, that's not how you do things. **Do serious politics with your homies, people who you really know,** if you want to do whatever. i'm just saying you should be careful about how you do politics because it changes your life one way or another. This is like a little lesson about how to do it or not do it." Well you see, nobody said this to these guys necessarily.

But who takes responsibility for these things? A movement really has to set up mechanisms. Just like there's a book fair here and people take responsibility for all the manifold functions, glorious and unglorious of the book fair. And if you have a movement people have to take responsibility for all its functions. Hey, security is one of these functions and it's not just being a marshal, and it's not just having a few official roles, right. It's a communal political activity.

Q : This question is because I have been thinking about the challenge of making good security compromises. For instance if you make use of a secure encrypted form of email, because you don't want to be monitored, that inconveniences you somewhat. And because there is a great deal of uncertainty about how closely we're being monitored and what the most secure ways of doing things are, we might be sort of shooting ourselves in the foot rather than just getting stuff done. You said earlier that the security stuff is part of a bigger picture of

*what we're trying to do, right. So if we make bad security com-
promises, we're actually going backwards a little bit. We go
backwards sometimes we go forwards sometimes, not every
decision we make has to be perfect. I read about security in
general (inaudible)... What do you think about, how do you
make good security compromises?*

J : Sorry, but i won't answer this question.(stir and comments
in audience) It's too big. It's a huge subject of trade-offs and
compromises, which can only be discussed in practical details.
So you and i would be going back and forth between ourselves
on this forever. i'm sorry, but it's too big for here.

*Q: Can you say what you mean in more detail by security itself,
like in a general sense. Because we keep saying it, and the
examples tend to help, but i thought it was about the art of
attack and defense, and we're always talking about defending
ourselves. Could you tell us what you mean by security?*

J: i'm not certain i quite understand, but the thing is this:
security is not just stopping infiltration. That's a big thing.
Because we're actually fighting in an area of the overall struggle, fighting capitalism and its state. Not as an idea or something far away that we protest, but in this area quite intimately.

When you go to school, there's a branch of capitalism that's
interested in selling you a tuition. And there's a branch of
capitalism that's interested in selling you shoes. And there's a
branch of capitalism that's interested in nullifying everything we
do as rebels and if necessary killing us, right?

Security is fighting that branch of capitalism. That's what it's
about. It's not basically defensive in nature. It's about the same
political struggle we do in our mass demonstrations, you know,
in actions or teaching, in whatever, when we go into this and
security blends into the edges of the larger struggle. That's why
when we start talking about these examples, they blend into
organizing and they blend into it because it's part of one political whole.

Q: in your presentation you talked a lot about infiltration, I was just wondering especially today how important you think that technique is versus acquiring information through surveillance of social media or photo video surveillance?

J: Well in reality today, they're both important. i mean the thing is maybe we think they don't need to infiltrate a group because they got it wiretapped and videotaped and everything only, that isn't how they think really. They really want their people there. It isn't just information in an abstract sense. The biggest problem they have politically is that they have information that they don't understand. And that's their biggest problem actually, when we fight. They need people to stir the mix, cook the dish.

This is a war, which means that we're never going to not have agents or infiltrators. That's like saying you'll have a war but you'll never have casualties, that's silly. Of course there'll be infiltrators. Just like they'll never stop us from reaching and influencing and winning over people on their side. Which we do.

i have a friend who convinced a cop to leave their side, to not be a cop. Had him as a student in Ethnic Studies, an Asian cop, and he got convinced—because it's pretty convincing that cops are the complete enemies of people of color and oppressed people. Just practically speaking, unless you really like shooting people who look like you, you know, who are poor and struggling, you shouldn't be a cop. And the last day of the course he came to my friend after the others had left, he thanked him for what he'd done, he unbelted his holster with his 9mm and gave it to my friend and said: *"If you ever need it for the movement, use it,"* and walked away. Serious.

So it isn't true—and look at Private Manning and all that—it isn't true that we're just on the defensive. We're fighting politically with them. We'll never stop them from doing some messing with us and causing us casualties and they won't stop us from winning people over.

So it's just like, when i came into the movement at 18 and didn't know anything but was glad to find others and do something political. And within a year i met people in or around the group who were agents. So earlier i've mentioned this one college drop-out guy acting like a Hollywood version of a revolutionary who turned out to be working for the FBI. There was another settler guy, his close "comrade" and friend in the group, who turned out to be a part-time informer for a county sheriff's office.

You know what i said about terrain, about knowing what the changes and moves in our terrain mean? Well, this second guy stood out like a dead spot to everyone because...he really hated us! i mean, hated us all personally, as people. He was a student at a conservative bible college, and he truly hated and feared all of us lefties so much that he couldn't even hide it. That stood out. He was acting like the pope trying to be undercover at a convention of Judas fans. Which made comrades think: why is a fundamentalist bible college student who seems to really hate almost everyone in the group even around us at all? There was nothing natural about it. Definitely, this second guy was a candidate for world's worst agent award.

It was so pathetic that comrades mostly laughed it off. And anyway, our social-democratic group wasn't exactly shaking capitalism from its foundations, we would have rejoiced and broken out the champagne bottles if we'd ever had any actual secrets to protect (yes, it was also true that any remotely sensitive discussions these clowns were kept away from).

So that "Dynamic Duo" was a good example of complete political police ineptitude, or a badly failed attempt at intelligence-gathering which we had deftly foiled? No, unfortunately, in the slippery long range of things it worked out in a way that shouldn't have surprised me but did.

James Yaki Sayles always told his New Afrikan comrades, over and over, "We have to take ourselves more seriously." This is a lesson which was really borne home to me, for instance, in this case. And, by the way, this relates to whether agent infiltration is so important to them anymore in an age of total electronic surveillance? This is a question that is raised all the time now not just by that comrade but whenever the issue of movement security comes up. The interesting fact is, our enemy has a "spare no expense" agenda when it comes to fighting the movement, weak though we are. They want it all, every tool, every weapon, and definitely **always see a priority need for human informers and agents.** We can make it plain.

While everyone in our little group back then laughed off these two obnoxious and obvious white guy agents, what we weren't thinking of was any larger picture. Like, to start with, if they were so isolated then how did they stay in contact with things at all? The answer was that they were part of a small dissident tendency led by one very smart comrade who wasn't considered an agent. Who was politically well educated from the IWW to Leninism, much more so than myself or most other young comrades. Let's call him "A". So what did that relationship mean? Well, "A" turned out to have a bad weakness which we saw but didn't see. His critical faculties got suspended whenever someone was willing to be his follower, to praise him and politically support his personal agendas. So "A" wasn't bothered by everyone's disbelief in the two agents in his clique.

While we dismissed them and laughed it off, the two fumbling agents had tripped over a very useful piece of information: "A" who was an experienced player in the left could be a security "aircraft carrier" for their whole team, a controversial though respected activist but one who could be manipulated to give political cover to more police infiltrators. How valuable that one piece of information could be.

"A" himself got deeper into the struggle over the years, being smart and curious and important. Wanting to be closer to "real" hard-core struggles such as Black nationalism and working class organizing and even supporting urban guerrilla politics in other countries. Inevitably, we now understand, as he got deeper into the struggle in at least one important situation he was used to run cover for and validate a police agent who outwardly was his "comrade". How often this happened we aren't completely sure, but the magic number isn't likely to be zero.

This is something those of us back in early days never understood or foresaw, because his major league egotism was just so "natural", so common for many of us in the movement back then that it didn't stand out. It was accepted as normal static on our political radios. Sometimes the most cutting secrets are the ones hidden in plain sight, hidden it turns out by our own hands from ourselves. **So human agents aren't just walking "ears" for the police. They are themselves catalysts as all people are, changing things and transforming things that might have not been otherwise.** The problem in the end turned out to be not with the two clumsy agents but with the smart and "political" comrade who wasn't thought to be dangerous like an agent would be—and we totally didn't see it coming.

What we do and don't do in our small spheres of political work, often has larger effects in the struggle far beyond us. Taking responsibility for that is hard.

Q: I wonder if you want to speak to... good politics is obviously a defense against infiltration and you gave a lot of examples that you can identify this person as an infiltrator because of their bad politics or because of our bad politics this person got a long way. But it also seems like branding people infiltrators, this is obviously really dangerous. I wonder if you could speak to some of the other preventative values of good politics or ways it may protect us that don't involve us identifying people as traitors, which is probably not even our biggest security problem.

J: It isn't. **Security is like all politics, all living. It's art and craft in as much as you need to know how to practically do it. You need experience at it.** You can't go around saying, "oh, you have bad politics, you're an agent", that's like harmful and silly, frankly. i don't want to get into too much tactical stuff because tactical stuff depends on the actual situation, it isn't a big principle that you're going to run out and apply like a cure-all lotion kind of thing. And when i talk about egotism or patriar-chy, in part that's because if i overemphasize it... in the sense that they seem to need cooler people as agents now, you know, who can fit in better. But of course in the '60s and '70s over and over and over again, we saw the same pattern. Only we couldn't stop ourselves. It was beyond our ability, because our politics weren't good enough. And not in any abstract way.

Like, you ask people how was Malcolm killed? If you say it was a conspiracy, then it must have been an operation and so how did it work, practically speaking? Malcolm had secu-rity and he had trained them, too. This is a guy who basically almost created the Fruit of Islam, the Nation of Islam's security people that cast a long shadow we all respected. So how did he get killed so easily in the Audubon Ballroom?

Answer: Eugene Roberts, police agent, who presented him-self as war veteran, top martial artist...like, "I like roughing up bad guys. Anybody who causes trouble with you, Malcolm, well don't worry. I won't let anyone … blah, blah, blah"…

Malcolm liked that. Sounded really tough, man-competent, you know? He made him head of security. So, did Eugene Roberts have good security? Absolutely—for *his* mission. He had painstaking security. Everybody who walked into the

Audubon Ballroom meetings was shaken down, patted down, their bags were emptied, you know, questioned, scrutinized, pushed around. Nobody was going to get past Eugene Roberts and his guys. After awhile, of course, many people stopped coming to Malcolm's speeches because they didn't feel like getting messed up and patted down on the way in, and people were complaining to Malcolm about it. So Malcolm said, "Well, this is counterproductive, this security thing!" So he said, "Okay, no more security, no more searching people at the door, no more patting everybody down, no more looking in their bags, just open the doors. It doesn't matter."

Bingo! Eugene Roberts struck the jackpot, got what he was aiming at with this murderous cop scheme. The minute he did that and then you got 3 dangerous other guys known to police coming into the weekly public meeting with shotgun and pistols. They came in and did the assassination in front of 200 people and 2 of the 3 got away. (One was grabbed by the crowd). Even though all of them were known to the state, the 2 who escaped were never caught or publicly named. Although the police did arrest innocent people afterwards, of course, as they usually do. Malcolm's security didn't do anything to protect him, because it wasn't *his* security anymore. New York police who were normally all over revolutionary meetings, disappeared for that night, totally not in sight. What a coincidence, they decided to take the night off. So it all worked out really well for the oppressors. Not so well for our side.

This happened to us over and over and over again in one way or another, coast to coast. It didn't happen just once, it happened 50, 100, 200, 300 times and you know something, we hardly learned a damn thing from it. So if people are beyond that and they know that, that's excellent—sorry it's just ABC's, but it cost us a lot to tell you this. i mean the knowledge, people died and only then did we get the knowledge in effect that we're dealing with. It's not nothing.

Q: I don't necessarily know if this is a positive example or not. I've had experience of groups I've been a part of having been infiltrated and I feel that one of the things that people have talked about a lot is about how much do you trust your gut? Like how do you go about trusting your gut if you think people are infiltrators without calling people out for being infiltrators when you could be wrong?

I would just caution people to not have just such a black-and-white ... you have suspicions about people so they're an informant and you treat them like a spy, but at the same time you don't react against that because of guilt and still include them in everything that you might not want to include them in. I think that people could take a more balanced approach to it and be straightforward about it and try not to alienate everyone they have suspicions of. I don't know what you think about that. It's something that we tried recently.

J: It's true, a lot of security questions when it comes to infiltration are gray, they're not black and white. Like most of them are gray. So you have to figure out how to deal with it. It depends on how much work you put into it. This may sound funny to you, but **we used to simply investigate people. It's not a big deal to me.**

Once the main anti-war group in Chicago was in a crisis because the guy who had the mailing list, they couldn't reach him by phone and they had to do an emergency mailing. So people went out to his house and they knocked on the door and he wasn't home. "Where the hell is this guy? he's a retired bookkeeper he told us, so where the heck is he? Oh, he's probably at the neighborhood tavern."

And so they went to the neighborhood tavern and said "Hey, you know so-and-so? Did you see him lately? You know, has he been here today?" And they said. "Oh, you mean so-and-so the cop?" And the anti-war people could only say, "What!?!" It turns out the guy was a full-time on duty Chicago police detective, right? He had the only copy of the movement mailing list for this citywide group...

They threatened him with a lawsuit to get the only copy of the mailing list back, but it sure changed things. Among other stuff, the comrades involved felt like fools. So they formed a small informal but no nonsense work group to not have it happen again. That wasn't a secret at all, but they didn't share all the details of the work with everyone, which was understood as just common sense. One of the techniques they used was they dug up a sympathizer who owned a small business, and had access to doing credit checks and bank info. Anyone they had questions about, they ran a credit check to see if their identity and work record matched with what they said about themselves. They also did other similar things, sometimes with unanticipated results. As well as checking with movement sources more. As an old Chinese philosopher once said, " No investigation, no right to speak."

And oh, here's another thing that came in our movement experience a lot: there were people, there wasn't anything on the surface wrong with them, they were nondescript, they sometimes didn't say anything at meetings. They'd say something fawning like: "Listen, I don't know too much about all these politics. I just wanna help and do your mailings , help do that kind of stuff." And some groups in the old days, hopefully not now, there was a hierarchy of roles: the important people didn't do any work, physical work, they gave orders and

*This new idea that the movement has to be completely transparent to everyone as a principle, especially to people whom we don't trust, to me **this is an unconscious influence from the liberal culture or something.** That no one should be held back from knowing everything that any part of the movement is up to? This is really new but not too fresh. To be blunt, this is an idea that has come about from the current distortion of the left as part of the cultural zone of "play nice" middle-class reformism. As though bourgeois civil liberties mindsets developed in part by interaction with cops and courts should define how we in the struggle relate and work with each other. As though we aren't outlaws and rebels. This didn't exist in earlier eras when the movement was primarily made up of oppressed working people fighting to survive, guarded in their trust, and for good reasons. "Necessity knows no laws."*

talked, whatever. And all the way down the hierarchy, the kind of new, "unimportant" people that nobody knew, they were left to do a lot of the practical whatnot.

It always sounded a little backwards to me, but anyways... So time and again, we just learned that this was like unbelievably backward on our parts...

When Roxanne Dunbar Ortiz left Boston's Cell 16, the first radical feminist group in the United States, to start a branch that they called the Southern Feminist Revolutionary Union or Women's Union or something like that in New Orleans, along the way they picked up this young woman who was a graduate student and who said as usual something like, "I love this feminism, I'm all for you, I don't talk much, I don't know much about it, but, you know, I just want to help. Like I'll do all the paperwork. I'll keep minutes of every meeting. I'll do all the correspondence. You creative leadership people, I want to free you to just go out and I'll just take care of little things."

So, of course, one day they came back to the office and discovered copies of letters that she had inadvertently left. It turns out of course, she really was a grad student and her professor apparently had been contacted by the FBI. So his line was, "Well, in order to get your thesis approved we want things like a psychological assessment of every person in this radical group. We want all their correspondence. We want to know their personal friends, etc, etc. We want to know this and we want to know that. This is all part of your thesis work. Just do this academic work and if you don't give us this we're throwing you out." She was a rich kid at a fancy university. So, of course she said "I have to do this". She was like a complete spy inside the group, but instead of being on the police payroll she was actually paying *them* lots of tuition money to get university credit for being a spy? You do know that capitalist culture is really weird, right?

This whole thing of hierarchy of roles thing, you know, really a bad idea, and not at all the same thing as practical division of labor. Working in the gray areas because we had to, we just looked up people, we thought about who they had worked with before. This wasn't a big witchhunt or anything. Just because we checked out peoples' stories and looked at people's background a lot because we had to, because we had bad experiences otherwise. This idea that we must automatically assume that everyone is good and trustworthy is just as crack as the idea that we must assume that everyone must be under suspicion and thought to be untrustworthy. Neither is realistic. We play the hand that we are dealt. And you do have to trust your gut and sometimes while you're working it out you put people in a bubble. They're in theory at the meeting, but actually you're working around them, you're protecting everyone from them but you're just not saying anything. i don't know, it sounds Machiavellian or whatever, but it's a war here. We're doing what we can, and if there are better ways then hopefully people will find them.

Q : I was just wondering, do we really need to figure out if someone is an agent or not, in order to figure out that they shouldn't be in one of our groups? One of those things that used to drive me nuts. Nobody wants to be the bad guy. That person is being sexist all the time, they shouldn't be in the group, right? A person who is disruptive so that we can't do our business during meetings shouldn't be in the group. I don't know, maybe it's different here, but a lot of people think it's the worst thing to be like, No you shouldn't be in this group. It's just really tough for some groups—maybe not every group—to say that somebody needs to take a time out.

J : Yes, you're right. Can't say any more than that.

Moderator: It's time, the meeting is over.

AN INTERVIEW WITH
MANDY HISCOCKS

Amanda "Mandy" Hiscocks is a long time activist from Guelph, Ontario. She was centrally involved in organizing against the G20 summit held in Toronto in June 2010. Tom Keefer interviewed Hiscocks a week before she was sentenced in January 2012. She served her sentence in the Vanier Center for Women in Milton, Ontario from where she maintained the blog http://boredbutnotbroken.tao.ca.

*   *   *   *   *   *   *   *   *

When and how did the police monitor organizers and infiltrate the movement against the G20?

They sent undercover agents in way before the G20 activism began. The two agents that I'm most familiar with—Brenda Dougherty (Brenda Carey) and Khalid Mohammed (Bindo Showan), in Guelph and Waterloo respectively—came in around the time of the planning against Vancouver Olympics. Their focus only morphed into G8/G20 surveillance later. But even before that, in 2008, I was placed under surveillance by the OPP because they claimed that I was involved in "extremist" left groups such as the Central Student Association (CSA) at the University of Guelph and People for the Ethical Treatment of Animals (PETA). I'm not a part of PETA and in any case, neither it nor the CSA are extremist groups.

What was perhaps more important for them was that they also said I was involved in "Aboriginal support" and that I was operating as a "bridge" between Guelph, Toronto, and

Ottawa. It's been a recurring theme in the Crown's synopsis of events to talk a lot about Indigenous solidarity work. I think the cops had people who were keeping tabs on activists in Guelph and Kitchener-Waterloo for their involvement in supporting Indigenous struggles and that they moved to a focus on the Olympics and the G20 when the Integrated Security Unit came into being.

What kind of Indigenous movements were you involved with that they were concerned about?

At the time, back in 2008, I would say nothing particularly structured. I had gone to some demonstrations and there was an Indigenous Peoples Solidarity Movement chapter in Guelph, but it wasn't particularly effective. I was going to a lot of events and helping to run events through the Ontario Public Research Interest Group (OPIRG). There was some Six Nations solidarity work going on at that time, and folks were also doing Tyendinaga support work. I would consider myself pretty peripheral to that work at that time, but as a whole the radical community in Guelph was very much into that kind of politics. I'm not really sure that I was actually a bridge between Toronto, Guelph, and Ottawa, but I did know a lot of people in those cities who were doing that kind of work. The main thing that the police were worried about was settler communities working with radical Indigenous people and they were also really worried about the more general networking that was happening in Southern Ontario. They didn't like that Kitchener, Guelph, and Hamilton were working really closely together and that there was a lot of anarchist organizing going on.

What kind of tactics and strategies did the state use to try to infiltrate the movement?

In my opinion, they did everything right. Khalid, the agent I'm most familiar with, came into Guelph and started working with the people opposing the Hanlon Creek Business Park development in Guelph. An above ground group called LIMITS, which held public meetings, organized petitions, spoke with city council, and hosted debates, had a big sign-up sheet, and wanted a really diverse group of people to join. Khalid started going to meetings and doing a lot of work, and then he met people in that group who were more connected to radical politics. There was crossover between that group and people who ended up doing an occupation at that site. He ended up at the occupation.

The occupation wasn't underground, but it was illegal. It was easy for him to slide into the other side of things. But at the same time, if we were to do it again, I'm not quite sure how we could prevent that. You do want lots of people joining your email lists and helping out, and if they seem solid, it's hard to justify keeping them out.

Were there things about his behaviour and activity that had people questioning whether or not he could be trusted or if he was a cop?

Yes, there were. I wasn't that involved in the Hanlon Creek occupation because I was on bail at the time and had a surety with money on the line, so I couldn't go to "unlawful" demonstrations, but I heard that there were people who didn't trust him. I'd hear people say, "Ugh, we can't be like this about people, just because he's brown and older, people need to calm down and not be so suspicious." So that debate was happening in Guelph, but eventually he did get kicked out of the occupation. I'm not sure about the circumstances, but I do know that it happened.

Then there was a backlash because he allied himself with an Indigenous man and a couple of other people at the occupation to identify the Guelph kids who kicked him out as racist. Either way, he did get kicked out and found his way to Kitchener and got involved in activism there. According to his notes in our disclosure, in Kitchener he established trust with a well known activist by doing things like buying illegal cigarettes from a nearby reserve and doing illegal drugs with other activists. He used the trust with that particular person to get into an organizing group in Kitchener.

What strategy did the police agent known as Brenda Dougherty use to get into the activist movement?

She came into Guelph in late 2008 or early 2009. She had instructions from her handlers at the OPP to go and just sit at the Cornerstone cafe because a lot of lefties hang around there; they thought that she should be seen in a cool, progressive coffee shop (she was getting paid to eat her lunch!). She read books like *Animal Rights and Human Wrongs* by Peter Singer and *One Dead Indian* by Peter Edwards. She watched the film *Trans America* and other really mainstream stuff to get a sense of the politics of the movement.

She had a list of people—targets—and she went to events, starting on campus, looking for people. She had photographs and was looking for "face time with targets," which is her own quote from the disclosure. She went to an International Women's Day event, did some other stuff, and eventually wound up at a Guelph Union of Tenants and Supporters (GUTS) meeting when they were trying to branch out and recruit on campus. Hardly anyone showed up to that meeting, so she was one of maybe four new members of the group. She started working with GUTS, which was doing very legal things like tenant advocacy and serving meals on the street. She got in by cooking and doing grunt work in a totally non-sketchy way. The cooking was done at people's houses and people became friendly and comfortable talking while she was in the room, and it transitioned into people talking about the G8/G20.

It wasn't even that activists were saying sketchy stuff, more just that she thought, "Okay, these are the people. I've hit the jackpot with this network, and I'm going to get to know these people a lot better and follow them." I don't know how she got to that first anti-G20 meeting in Guelph. I was protesting at the Olympics in Vancouver at the time, so I don't know if it was an open meeting or if she had been invited because she was around for long enough that people trusted her. But she ended up at the first meeting of what would become the Southern Ontario Anarchist Resistance (SOAR) before there was a vouch system in place. And then she breezed through all the rest. I don't think anyone ever sat down and asked, "Who here is officially vouching for Brenda?" But when there was an official vouch system, I vouched for her at a meeting months later—to my eternal shame. I think she got in because she had done so much work and had been there from the start.

One of the conditions of your bail prevented any of the co-accused from contacting one another. In retrospect, do you think it made sense for you to have accepted the nonassociation conditions that were required to get out of custody after you were first arrested?

Well, I can say that I'm never doing that again. I will not take nonassociation conditions again, and I will not go into an arrestable action without understanding that I could be in jail for months and months. I can't speak for other people, but I think that what set the tone for the conditions we got, more than anything, was the fact that we had lawyers. The lawyers wanted to get us out at any cost and were willing to agree to pretty much anything. If we had refused lawyers, they wouldn't have been able to put non-association restrictions on us, because we would have had to communicate for the trial.

Ideally, we should have said, "We all get out (or not) but we have to have a way to meet." If we had stayed in jail, all the women would have been able to meet together and all the men would have been able to meet together. We were all on the same ranges. We would have had a little bit more time to have conversations. The way it turned out, we never had time to talk. We weren't a group of 17 people with a plan, so we didn't have time to properly discuss things like, "How do you feel about non-association?" since we'd never done that kind of pre-arrest stuff that you do if you're doing a cohesive action with a group of people. If we had not signed the non-association agreement and if we had stayed in jail, we could have done that.

I remember arguing with my lawyer about this, and he was adamant: "No, no, this is okay. They're just playing it up because of the media, everything will die down, just keep your heads down and in a few months we'll sort it out." And I should not have believed him! It's been my experience that it's really hard to change bail conditions later. Most people in jail wanted to get out quickly. We didn't have a real discussion in jail that I can remember about whether we should stay there and work as a group to get better conditions later. People hadn't prepared for that. People had stuff at home that was hanging over them, people had work, people hadn't thought this stuff through.

What about the publication ban?

Once our lawyers got the publication ban in place it was really hard for people to know what they could do on our behalf, and it also meant there were a lot of complications with organizing any kind of protest. One problem was that people didn't know what they could say, or even if they could say anything. Another was that there is this weird kind of loophole in the conspiracy law that seemed to mean that if you were alleged to have been part of the conspiracy, and if at a later date in court you were deemed to have actually been a part of that conspiracy, then anything that you said, even after your arrest, is assumed to have been said by anyone in the group. So, everyone was scared to speak without the consent of the group, which we couldn't get because we had non-association conditions. There was also this idea of the "unindicted co-conspirator," someone who hasn't been arrested but is considered by the Crown to be part of the conspiracy. That loophole would also apply to them, so no one who thought they might be an unindicted co-conspirator wanted to speak either. It was surreal and confusing. We didn't understand it and we couldn't get a straight legal answer. Someone needs to study this stuff and see what the law actually says and what the restrictions are, so that we know it better for next time.

What do you think the level of fallout has been on the activists involved in G20 organizing? Have people been scared off or has this process strengthened people's understanding of what's at stake and what's required?

I really don't know. I know what I'd like to think: I'd like to think that people are having better conversations about what they're willing to do, about what they're willing to give up. One of the goals of the TCMN (Toronto Community Mobilization Network) was to use the G20 to get people excited and to join groups that were organizing in the city. To some extent I think that happened.

I also think that if you were one of the people who got attacked at Queen's Park on June 26, you have a pretty different understanding of riot police now. That can be a powerful moment, when you see the state for what it really is. Hopefully people who were there have a better understanding of the state and the police, where they fit, and what the right to protest really means. Hopefully it made people angrier and not more fearful of state repression. But I don't have a good way of knowing if that's the case. In terms of prison solidarity, it's done wonders. The number of people, even just people connected to me on Facebook, who are involved in letter writing, posting

information about Bill C-101* and programs in prisons, and dis-
seminating information that they wouldn't normally, has grown
exponentially. I don't know if that's taking away from other work,
but it seems that there is more of a focus on prisoners as a
political issue.

*How would you respond to the critique that a proponent of
non-violent direct action might make, where everything should
be organized transparently and people should only engage in
civil disobedience so that no one can be portrayed as a terrorist or as being violent? Has that made you reconsider your
position on questions around violence or fighting the cops?*

No, not at all. I would have liked everything to unfold as a cross
between an autonomous black bloc and the way that affinity
groups were organized in the anti-globalization movement days.
Like the pie chart in Seattle, divide the city: "Is there an affinity group that can shut down this part of the city? Hands up,
awesome, there's ten of you, great. Do you need more people,
no? Okay, go to it, go do your autonomous thing." The idea
behind SOAR was that it would allow for a little more coopera-
tion between affinity groups so that there weren't just a random
bunch of affinity groups doing whatever. If one affinity group
was doing a particular thing, maybe another affinity group could
assist, through a complementary action, or use their own action
as a decoy and so on. That's not the way it panned out, but
that was the idea that I had and that was the idea behind the
spokescouncils of affinity groups that made up SOAR.

In the end, all of the "ring-leaders" in SOAR were in jail and
completely different people took the lead on the day of the
march and put up a flare and a bunch of people followed them.
It was just a standard black bloc: people wearing black, people
who knew and trusted one another, and they went and engaged
in some "criminal activity." The militant action ended up being
less organized but it happened and I think it accomplished

——— ——— ——— ——— ——— ———

* Omnibus Crime Bill C-10, also called the "Safer Streets, Safer
Communities Act," was passed by the Canadian federal government in March 2012. The bill combines amendments from nine
separate bills that had failed to pass in previous sessions of par-
liament and makes fundamental changes to almost every compo-
nent of Canada's criminal justice system.

what it was meant to. And all of that organization that went into SOAR, all of the time and the energy, maybe it was unnecessary. I don't mean that the idea of more coordinated affinity group actions should be abandoned, or that it's a bad model, just that it didn't work this time and we need to think it through more.

If the state of the movement right now was such that another Seattle could happen, or that there were affinity groups out there who acted with no bandanas, who did things like hard blockades, who knew how to do those things, who had the equipment, and were willing do them, I think we would have had a really different situation. The assessment that I and that most people have, however, is that that doesn't exist anymore. People don't do those things. It's not the Pacific Northwest, it's not the anti-logging stuff, it's not the anti-globalization days.

I walked into those meetings in Toronto and looked around and thought, where is everyone? Where are the people who have these skills, who know how to do this stuff? They weren't there. And I remember speaking with a friend of mine who is completely pacifist, and does only non-violent direct action and does it really well and coordinated and I was asked, "Are you going to be here? Can we have some yellow actions?" But there just weren't those things. I think that's a problem. Because we have really boring, not very useful, union/NGO-style marches or black bloc actions and nothing in the middle.

It's important to note that it wasn't only the radical anarchists who were infiltrated. Greenpeace and the Vancouver Media Centre were infiltrated too. A lot of pretty mainstream groups who do mostly non-violent civil disobedience (if they do anything illegal at all) were infiltrated. I don't think it's true that the infiltration wouldn't have happened if there wasn't this idea of "violence."

It seems that in some ways that black bloc actions have become symbolic actions in themselves and that "it's not a good summit protest unless something is burning." The act of smashing stuff is seen as a victory in itself, even though it's really symbolic and ultimately resulted in the trouble that you and a number of other people went through—all the trials and all the jail time.

The thing is, we knew that the black bloc was going to happen, because it always happens. SOAR or no SOAR, there's going to be a black bloc. And so the question that we had—in SOAR and the TCMN—was how can we use diversity of tactics to separate the labour march from another march where people can be more "militant." The original idea was always that shit is going to happen—it always happens and organizers can't and shouldn't control what people are going to do or not going to do.

It's a fair bet that there's going to be a black bloc and there are going to be smashed windows. How do we make sure that that happens in a place and in a way that doesn't affect the green march or the low-risk march? That was the intention and it didn't work out that way, and it kind of didn't work out that way because of a lack of respect for a diversity of tactics. If there had been a friendly, cordial, "We don't agree but we recognize that some people want to do different things," message from the labour march, I think it would have turned out really well.

As for the value of having a small black bloc that runs amok in the city—I haven't decided either way on that. I think there is some value to showing any kind of resistance that is militant, that's in your face, that says, "No, you can't scare me with your tear gas. You can't scare me with your guns. Fuck you." I think that's really important in ways that can't necessarily be assessed. And I don't think the window smashing matters. I don't think the smashing cop cars matters. I think that whatever gives an aura of militancy in the street is really valuable.

I don't know that a civil disobedience "lie down and let's get dragged away" action does do that. I think it does a lot of other great things, but it doesn't inspire the same people as a more confrontational action does. When I was in jail, the general consensus on my range was, "That was fucking awesome." People who have been constantly harassed by cops, whether they have a really good class analysis or just plain experience, thought it was great. People who hate the power structure but don't really have a background or academic understanding of it were drawn to the militant actions, and that's what's positive. So I don't think the bloc should be assessed in terms of people getting arrested, or whether or not we shut it down, or if the unions are mad at us now.

I just wish that there had also been a middle ground. I wish that there were people saying, "We're going to lie down on the Gardiner Expressway," or saying, "We're not going to let the delegates through," or "We're going to put a tripod in the middle of the entrance way," or "We're going to lock down at the fence."

One thing that I learned was that you can either be part of organizing the structure—making the posters, making the timelines, getting the convergence space—or you can be part of a group that's going to be doing an action, but you can't do both. There is no way that my affinity group could have actually planned a really solid action while we were also doing all of the structure stuff. That was the main drawback: that there were not enough people in the city that were willing to give enough of their time to allow people who were part of the TCMN to also plan actions. In hindsight, we needed the people in the TCMN to just plan a big militant action. No one else was doing it and SOAR ended up taking it on.

It's almost a reflection of the fact that the balance of forces has changed since Seattle and the G20 in Toronto.

It seems that there are fewer people participating, and that people from both sides of the "violence" debate are scornful of the middle. There are people who are only willing to march and will not do anything illegal. And then there are people who are like, "Fuck this non-violent direct action shit, I want to break some windows. I want to do something that feels strong and empowering. I'm going to dress all in black and be part of the black bloc."

Neither side is interested in the classic mass civil disobedience actions. If there was a middle force between these extremes, maybe there would be more people and if there were more people, maybe there would be a middle.

But yeah—it's definitely different. But it's not just time; I think it's also location. I think if the G20 had happened, for example, in Montreal, where there's a different political culture, it would have been totally different. There you can be part of a militant march that will confront the police, or at least defend itself against the police. Folks there who will attack a fence or a structure and do that kind of thing on a regular basis don't dress all in black in some kind of cliquey subculture. If the G20 had met in Montreal, I don't think the weird conflict between the union and the break-off march would have happened. People would have said, "Of course we will do a militant break-off march."

My really over-simplified analysis of the black bloc—or the kinds of things the black bloc would do—is that we've been doing it backwards. For the last decade, since Seattle, people have been trying to normalize the black bloc. Our thinking was that the more we do it the more people will get used to it and the more appealing these tactics will become.

But we should be looking at Egypt. The protests in Tahrir Square were always called peaceful protests. There was the classic "women and children" line: it was peaceful and it was meant to be peaceful and in the interviews everyone said how peaceful it was and that they just wanted a peaceful demonstration that was massive, to just make their point. But when the police and Mubarak's people attacked there was not a lot of conflict or tension when people started defending the square and the protest against the state's forces. Hundreds of people were doing things like burning down police stations as well as climbing on top of tall buildings and throwing molotovs down when the cops came!

It's almost as if black bloc activists need to bide their time, practice their tactics, but not in a public way because the only time it's going to be acceptable here is when people feel threatened. If the cops had attacked the labour march I don't know that the unions would have been so upset about a bunch of people fighting the cops; maybe then they might have thought, "Oh yeah—this is okay. My four year old is here and it's great that this person in black is preventing the cops from getting too close." People almost do politics as a hobby, like, "Let's go out for the day and march around with the unions," so they might not see the value of the black bloc. But they would if they faced the risk of police violence themselves. Because non-violent rallies are not a threat to the state, the state doesn't respond with violence. And in my mind, a defensive black bloc that contributes to a larger action is more useful than one that goes alone and engages in small scale property damage.

As you prepare to do 11 months in jail, is there anything that you want to tell people, or are there ways that people can support you in jail, or ways that you can work with prisoner support movements?

The one thing I would like to tell people—because I think people have a really skewed perception of what jail is—is that it's not really going to be that terrible. I think that it's really important for people to know that this is something we can do. People have this idea that jail is to be avoided at all costs and it's the end of the world if you have to do time. I'm hoping that my experience, when I can share it, will demonstrate that it's not so bad. You can still do important things on the inside and you will still have contact with the outside and it doesn't take a particularly strong person to be able to get through it.

So you see it as part of the political process, if we're serious about changing the world?

Exactly. It's not like they're going to stop arresting people. However, there are only so many times that you can do time in your life, so I think those times should be worth it. If you are going to put yourself out there knowing that you could potentially do time, then just make sure that your actions are as efficient and effective as possible.

MORE FROM KERSPLEBEDEB

ALL POWER TO THE PEOPLE
ALBERT "NUH" WASHINGTON
1894820215 • 111 pp. • $10.00

A collection of writings by the late Albert Nuh Washington, a former member of the Black Panther Party and Black Liberation Army. One of the "New York 3", Washington was imprisoned in 1971 as a result of the U.S. government's war against the Black Liberation Movement; he died in prison almost thirty years later, on April 28, 2000, from cancer. (2002)

AMAZON NATION OR ARYAN NATION: WHITE WOMEN AND THE COMING OF BLACK GENOCIDE
BOTTOMFISH BLUES • 9781894946551
160 pp. • $12.95

The massive New Afrikan uprisings of the 1960s were answered by the white ruling class with the destruction of New Afrikan communities coast to coast, the decimation of the New Afrikan working class, the rise of the prison state and an explosion of violence between oppressed people. Taken on their own, in isolation, these blights may seem to be just more "social issues" for NGOs to get grants for, but taken together and in the context of amerikkkan history, they constitute genocide. (2014)

A SOLDIER'S STORY: REVOLUTIONARY WRITINGS BY A NEW AFRIKAN ANARCHIST THIRD EDITION
KUWASI BALAGOON • 9781629633770
272 PP. • $19.95

Kuwasi Balagoon was a participant in the Black Liberation struggle from the 1960s until his death in prison in 1986. A member of the Black Panther Party and defendant in the infamous Panther 21 case, Balagoon went underground with the Black Liberation Army (BLA). Captured and convicted of various crimes against the State, he spent much of the 1970s in prison, escaping twice. After each escape, he went underground and resumed BLA activity. This is the most complete collection of his writings, poetry, and court statements ever collected, along with recollections from those who knew him, and who have been inspired by him since his passing. (2019)

AUSTERITY APPARATUS
J. MOUFAWAD-PAUL • 9781894946551
160 pp. • $12.95

An excavation of the ideology of austerity and its relationship to the mechanisms of capitalism, a philosophical excursion through a variety of concepts surrounding capitalist crisis and class struggle. Written as a series of interconnected meditations on the problematic of austerity, Austerity Apparatus is a creative intervention rather than a polemic or rigorous analysis; it is designed to force reflection on the ways in which contemporary capitalism conditions its subjects to accept its limits. (2017)

BEGINNER'S KATA: UNCENSORED STRAY THOUGHTS ON REVOLUTIONARY ORGANIZATION

J. SAKAI • NO ISBN • 15 pp. • $3.00

Plain talk with J. Sakai about what we do and don't know about revolutionary organization, and, indeed, about being revolutionaries. (2018)

CATEGORIES OF REVOLUTIONARY MILITARY POLICY

T. DERBENT • 9781894946438 • 52 pp. • $5.00

An educational survey of the concepts of military doctrine, strategy, tactics, operational art, bases of support, guerilla zones, liberated territories, and more. A study of what has been tried in the past, where different strategies worked, and where they failed, all from a perspective concerned with making revolution. (2013)

CHICAN@ POWER AND THE STRUGGLE FOR AZTLAN

CIPACTLI & EHECATL • 9781894946742 320 pp. • $22.95

From the Amerikan invasion and theft of Mexican lands, to present day migrants risking their lives to cross the U.$. border, the Chican@ nation has developed in a cauldron of national oppression and liberation struggles. This book by a MIM(Prisons) Study Group presents the history of the Chicano movement, exploring the colonialism and semi-colonialism that frames the Chican@ national identity. It also sheds new light on the modern repression and temptation that threaten liberation struggles by simultaneously pushing for submission and assimilation into Amerika. (2015)

THE COMMUNIST NECESSITY 2ND EDITION

J. MOUFAWAD-PAUL • PREFACE BY DAO-YUAN CHOU 9781989701003 • 171 pp. • $12.00

A polemical interrogation of the practice of "social movementism" that has enjoyed a normative status at the centres of capitalism. Aware of his past affinity with social movementism, and with some apprehension of the problem of communist orthodoxy, the author argues that the recognition of communism's necessity "requires a new return to the revolutionary communist theories and experiences won from history." This second edition of Moufawad-Paul's first book includes a preface by Dao-yuan Chou and a reflective afterword by the author. (2020)

CONFRONTING FASCISM: DISCUSSION DOCUMENTS FOR A MILITANT MOVEMENT, SECOND EDITION 2017

XTN, D. HAMERQUIST, J. SAKAI, M. SALOTTE 9781894946872 • 219 pp. • $14.95

Essays grappling with the class appeal of fascism, its continuities and breaks with the "regular" far-right and also even with the Left. Written from the perspective of revolutionaries active in the struggle against the far right. (2002)

THE DANGEROUS CLASS AND REVOLUTIONARY THEORY: THOUGHTS ON THE MAKING OF THE LUMPEN/PROLETARIAT

J. SAKAI • 9781894946902 • 308 pp. • $24.95

As detailed in the first part of this book, while at first dismissing them in the Communist Manifesto as "that passively rotting mass" at the obscure lower depths, Marx soon realized that the lumpen could be players at the very center of events in revolutionary civil war. Even at the center in the startling rise of new regimes. Next, in the paper "Mao Z's Revolutionary Laboratory and the

Role of the Lumpen Proletariat," Sakai shows how the left's euro-centrism here prevented it from realizing the obvious: that the basic theory from European radicalism about the lumpen/proletariat was first fully tested not there or here but in the Chinese Revolution of 1921–1949. One could hardly wish for a larger test tube, and the many lessons to be learned from this mass political experience are finally put on the table. (2017)

DEFYING THE TOMB: SELECTED PRISON WRITINGS AND ART OF KEVIN "RASHID" JOHNSON FEATURING EXCHANGES WITH AN OUTLAW
KEVIN "RASHID" JOHNSON • 9781894946391 386 pp. • $20.00

Follow the author's odyssey from lumpen drug dealer to prisoner, to revolutionary New Afrikan, a teacher and mentor, one of a new generation rising of prison intellectuals. (2010)

DIVIDED WORLD DIVIDED CLASS: GLOBAL POLITICAL ECONOMY AND THE STRATIFICATION OF LABOUR UNDER CAPITALISM, SECOND EDITION 2015
ZAK COPE • 9781894946681 • 460 pp. • $24.95

The history of the 'labour aristocracy' in the capitalist world system, from its roots in colonialism to its birth and eventual maturation into a full-fledged middle class in the age of imperialism. Pervasive national, racial and cultural chauvinism in the core capitalist countries is not primarily attributable to 'false class consciousness' or ignorance as much left and liberal thinking assumes. Rather, these and related forms of bigotry are concentrated expressions of the major social strata of the core capitalist nations' shared economic interest in the exploitation and repression of dependent nations.(2012)

EUROCENTRISM AND THE COMMUNIST MOVEMENT
ROBERT BIEL • 9781894946711 • 215 pp. • $17.95

A work of intellectual history, Eurocentrism and the Communist Movement explores the relationship between Eurocentrism, alienation, and racism, while tracing the different ideas about imperialism, colonialism, "progress", and non-European peoples as they were grappled with by revolutionaries in both the colonized and colonizing nations. Teasing out racist errors and anti-racist insights within this history, Biel reveals a century-long struggle to assert the centrality of the most exploited within the struggle against capitalism. The roles of key figures in the Marxist-Leninist canon—Marx, Engels, Lenin, Stalin, Mao—within this struggle are explored, as are those of others whose work may be less familiar to some readers, such as Sultan Galiev, Lamine Senghor, Lin Biao, R.P. Dutt, Samir Amin, and others. (2015)

EXODUS AND RECONSTRUCTION: WORKING-CLASS WOMEN AT THE HEART OF GLOBALIZATION
BROMMA • 9781894946421 • 37 pp. • $3.00

The position of women at the heart of a transformed global proletariat: "Family-based rural patriarchy was so deeply imbedded within capitalism for so long that abandoning it was nearly unthinkable. A change of such magnitude would require the development of much more advanced global transportation and commodity markets and a tremendous reorganization of labor. It would require a major overhaul of political systems everywhere. It would be a sea-change in capitalism. That sea-change is what's happening now." (2013)

FALSE NATIONALSM
FALSE INTERNATIONALISM:
CLASS CONTRADICTIONS
IN THE ARMED STRUGGLE
E. TANI AND KAÉ SERA • 978-1-989701-08-9
327 pp. • $26.95

A critical history of revisionism, opportunism, and parasitical relationships between white and Black revolutionary organizations in the United States. Chapters address important aspects of the Russian and Chinese revolutions; different forms of solidarity with the antifascist resistance in Spain and Ethiopia; the racist settlerist machinations of the CPUSA; relationships between revolutionaries in the New Left, including the Weather Underground and the Black Panther Party; and, finally, the tragic experiences of the Revolutionary Armed Task Force. This book first appeared in 1985 as an attempt to evaluate the rise in radical armed activity in the US during the 1960s and 1970s from an activist perspective. (2021)

FULL BODY SCAN:
IMPERIALISM TODAY
GABRIEL KUHN & BROMMA • 9781894946957
36 pp. • $4.00

Gabriel Kuhn's "Oppressor and Oppressed Nations: Sketching a Taxonomy of Imperialism", with a response from Bromma, debating the nature of nations, nation-states, and countries, and the distribution of privilege and potential in the world today. (2018)

THE GLOBAL PERSPECTIVE:
REFLECTIONS ON IMPERIALISM
AND RESISTANCE
TORKIL LAUESEN • 9781894946933 • 544 pp. • $24.95

Bridging the gap between Third Worldist theory and the question of "What Is To Be Done?" in a First World context, The Global Perspective is an important contribution towards developing an effective political practice based on the realities of the global situation, avoiding the pitfalls of sugarcoating the situation with the First World populations, or of falling into pessimistic quietism. As Lauesen says, "It is a book written by an activist, for activists. Global capitalism is heading into a deep structural crisis in the coming decades, so the objective conditions for radical change will be present, for better or for worse. The outcome will depend on us, the subjective forces." (2018)

THE GREEN NAZI: AN
INVESTIGATION
INTO FASCIST ECOLOGY
J. SAKAI • 0968950396 • 34 pp. • $3.00

A review of Blood and Soil, a book by academic Anna Bramwell, disputing her flattering portrayal of Third Reich Imperial Peasant Leader Walther Darre. A critical look at the relationship between social and natural purity, the green movement and the far right. (2002)

THE HISTORICAL FAILURE OF
ANARCHISM: IMPLICATIONS
FOR THE FUTURE OF THE
REVOLUTIONARY PROJECT
CHRISTOPHER DAY • 9781894946452 • 26 pp. • $4.00

An exposition of the failure of anarchism to successfully carry out or defend revolution in the 20th century, raising questions for the future. (2009)

INSURGENT SUPREMACISTS:
THE U.S. FAR RIGHT'S
CHALLENGE TO STATE AND
EMPIRE
MATTHEW LYONS • 9781629635118 • 384 pp. • $24.95

A major study of movements that strive to overthrow the U.S. government, that often claim to be anti-imperialist and sometimes even anti-capitalist yet also consciously promote inequality, hierarchy, and domination, generally along explicitly racist, sexist, and homophobic lines. Revolutionaries of the far right: insurgent supremacists. Intervening directly in debates within left and antifascist movements, Lyons examines both the widespread use and abuse of the term "fascism," and the relationship between federal security forces and the paramilitary right. His final chapter offers a preliminary analysis of the Trump presidential administration relationship with far-right politics and the organized far right's shifting responses to it. (2018)

IS CHINA AN IMPERIALIST COUNTRY?

N.B. TURNER ET AL. • 9781894946759 • 173 pp. • $17.00

Whether or not China is now a capitalist-imperialist country is an issue on which there is some considerable disagreement, even within the revolutionary left. This book brings together theoretical, definitional and logical considerations, as well as the extensive empirical evidence that is now available, to demonstrate that China has indeed definitely become a capitalist-imperialist country. (2015)

JAILBREAK OUT OF HISTORY: THE RE-BIOGRAPHY OF HARRIET TUBMAN (2ND EDITION)

BUTCH LEE • 9781894946704 • 169 pp. • $14.95

Anticolonial struggles of New Afrikan/Black women were central to the unfolding of 19th century amerika, both during and "after" slavery. "The Re-Biography of Harriet Tubman", recounts the life and politics of Harriet Tubman, who waged and eventually lead the war against the capitalist slave system. "The Evil of Female Loaferism" details New Afrikan women's attempts to withdraw from and evade capitalist colonialism, an unofficial but massive labor strike which threw the capitalists North and South into a panic. The ruling class response consisted of the "Black Codes", Jim Crow, re-enslavement through prison labor, mass violence, and ... the establishment of a neo-colonial Black patriarchy, whose task was to make New Afrikan women subordinate to New Afrikan men just as New Afrika was supposed to be subordinate to white amerika. (2015)

KARL MARX AND FRIEDRICH ENGELS: ON COLONIES, INDUSTRIAL MONOPOLY AND THE WORKING CLASS MOVEMENT

INTRODUCTION BY ZAK COPE & TORKIL LAUESEN
9781894946797 • 160 pp. • $10.00

Selections from Marx and Engels, showing the evolution of their ideas on the nascent labor aristocracy and the complicating factors of colonialism and chauvinism, with a focus on the British Empire of their time. In their introduction, Cope and Lauesen show how Marx and Engels' initial belief that capitalism would extend seamlessly around the globe in the same form was proven wrong by events, as instead worldwide imperialism spread capitalism as a polarizing process, not only between the bourgeoisie and the working class, but also as a division between an imperialist center and an exploited periphery. (2016)

LEARNING FROM AN UNIMPORTANT MINORITY

J. SAKAI • 9781894946605 • 118 pp. • $10.00

Race is all around us, as one of the main structures of capitalist society. Yet, how we talk about it and even how we think about it is tightly policed. Everything about race is artificially distorted as a white/Black paradigm. Instead, we need to understand the imposed racial reality from many different angles of radical vision. In this talk given at the 2014 Montreal Anarchist Bookfair, J. Sakai shares experiences from his own life as a revolutionary in the united states, exploring what it means to belong to an "unimportant minority." (2015)

LOOKING AT THE U.S. WHITE WORKING CLASS HISTORICALLY
DAVID GILBERT • 9781894946919 • 97 pp. • $10.00

On the one hand, "white working class" includes a class designation that should imply, along with all other workers of the world, a fundamental role in the overthrow of capitalism. On the other hand, there is the identification of being part of a ("white") oppressor nation. Political prisoner David Gilbert seeks to understand the origins of this contradiction, its historical development, as well as possibilities to weaken and ultimately transform the situation. (2017)

LUMPEN: THE AUTOBIOGRAPHY OF ED MEAD
ED MEAD • 9781894946780 • 360 pp. • $20.00

When a thirteen-year-old Ed Mead ends up in the Utah State Industrial School, a prison for boys, it is the first step in a story of oppression and revolt that will ultimately lead to the foundation of the George Jackson Brigade, a Seattle-based urban guerrilla group, and to Mead's re-incarceration as a fully engaged revolutionary, well-placed and prepared to take on both his captors and the predators amongst his fellow prisoners. This is his story, and there is truly nothing like it. (2015)

MEDITATIONS ON FRANTZ FANON'S WRETCHED OF THE EARTH: NEW AFRIKAN REVOLUTIONARY WRITINGS
JAMES YAKI SAYLES • 9781894946322 • 399 pp. • $20.00

One of those who eagerly picked up Fanon in the 60s, who carried out armed expropriations and violence against white settlers, Sayles reveals how behind the image of Fanon as race thinker there is an underlying reality of antiracist communist thought. From the book: "This exercise is about more than our desire to read and understand Wretched (as if it were about some abstract world, and not our own); it's about more than our need to understand (the failures of) the anti-colonial struggles on the African continent. This exercise is also about us, and about some of the things that We need to understand and to change in ourselves and our world." (2010)

THE MILITARY STRATEGY OF WOMEN AND CHILDREN
BUTCH LEE • 0973143231 • 116 pp. • $12.00

Lays out the need for an autonomous and independent women's revolutionary movement, a revolutionary women's culture that involves not only separating oneself from patriarchal imperialism, but also in confronting, opposing, and waging war against it by all means necessary. (2003)

MY ENEMY'S ENEMY: ESSAYS ON GLOBALIZATION, FASCISM AND THE STRUGGLE AGAINST CAPITALISM
ANTI-FASCIST FORUM • 0973143231 • 116 pp. • $10.00

Articles by anti-fascist researchers and political activists from Europe and North America, examining racist and pro-capitalist tendencies within the movement against globalization. (2003)

NIGHT-VISION: ILLUMINATING WAR AND CLASS ON THE NEO-COLONIAL TERRAIN SECOND EDITION 2017
BUTCH LEE AND RED ROVER • 9781894946889 264 pp. • $17.00

"The transformation to a neo-colonial world has only begun, but it promises to be as drastic, as disorienting a change as was the original european colonial conquest of the human race. Capitalism is again ripping apart & restructuring the world, and nothing will be the same. Not race, not nation, not gender, and certainly not whatever culture you used to have. Now you have outcast groups as diverse as the Aryan Nation and the Queer Nation

and the Hip Hop Nation publicly rejecting the right of the u.s. government to rule them. All the building blocks of human culture—race, gender, nation, and especially class—are being transformed under great pressure to embody the spirit of this neo-colonial age." (2009)

1978: A NEW STAGE IN THE CLASS WAR?
SELECTED DOCUMENTS ON THE SPRING CAMPAIGN OF THE RED BRIGADES
ED. JOSHUA DEPAOLIS • 9781894946995 218 pp. • $19.95

For the first time in English, a selection of the key documents on the strategic logic and conjunctural analysis behind the 1978 offensive of the Red Brigades, the kidnapping and execution of Italy's President Aldo Moro, which brought the BR's strategy of "attack on the heart of the state" to a climax and induced a national political crisis. (2019)

NOTES TOWARD AN UNDERSTANDING OF CAPITALIST CRISIS & THEORY
J. SAKAI • 1894946316 • 25 pp. • $2.00

An examination of Marx's theories of capitalist crisis, in light of the current economic crisis, asking some tentative questions of what it all might mean in terms of strategy, and things to come. (2009)

ON THE VANGUARD ONCE AGAIN...
KEVIN "RASHID" JOHNSON 9781894946445 • 23 pp. • $4.00

A response to anarchist criticisms of Marxism-Leninism, defending the concepts of the vanguard party and democratic centralism, from the perspective of the New Afrikan Black Panther Party Prison Chapter. (2013)

OUR COMMITMENT IS TO OUR COMMUNITIES: MASS INCARCERATION, POLITICAL PRISONERS, AND BUILDING A MOVEMENT FOR COMMUNITY-BASED JUSTICE
DAVID GILBERT • 9781894946650 • 34 pp. • $5.00

In this pamphlet, interviewed by Bob Feldman, political prisoner David Gilbert discusses the ongoing catastrophe that is mass incarceration, connecting it to the continued imprisonment of political prisoners and the challenges that face our movements today. (2014)

PANTHER VISION
KEVIN "RASHID" JOHNSON • 9781894946766 496 pp. • $24.95

Essential Party Writings and Art of Kevin "Rashid" Johnson, Minister of Defense, New Afrikan Black Panther Party-Prison Chapter. Subjects addressed include the differences between anarchism and Marxism-Leninsm, the legacy of the Black Panther Party, the timeliness of Huey P. Newton's concept of revolutionary intercommunalism, the science of dialictical and historical materialsm, the practice of democratic centralism, as well as current events ranging from u.s. imperialist designs in Africa to national oppression of New Afrikans within u.s. borders. And much more. (2015)

THE PRINCIPAL CONTRADICTION
TORKIL LAUESEN • 9781989701034 • 157 pp. • $14.95

An introduction the philosophy of dialectical materialism as a tool for changing the world. Dialectical materialism allows us to understand the dynamics of world history, the concept of contradiction building a bridge between theory and practice, with the principal contradiction telling us where to start. Identifying the principal contradiction is indispensable for developing a global perspective on capitalism. This *methodology is not just a valuable tool with which to analyze complex relationships: it also tells us how to intervene. (2020)*

PRISON ROUND TRIP

KLAUS VIEHMANN • PREFACE BY BILL DUNNE
9781604860825 • 25 pp. • $3.00

First published in German in 2003 as "Einmal Knast und zurück." The essay's author, Klaus Viehmann, had been released from prison ten years earlier, after completing a 15-year sentence for his involvement in urban guerilla activities in Germany in the 1970s. Here he reflects on how to keep one's sanity and political integrity within the hostile and oppressive prison environment; "survival strategies" are its central theme. (2009)

THE RED ARMY FACTION, A DOCUMENTARY HISTORY, VOLUME 1: PROJECTILES FOR THE PEOPLE

ANDRE MONCOURT & J. SMITH EDS.
9781604860290 • 736 pp. • $34.95

For the first time ever in English, this volume presents all of the manifestos and communiqués issued by the RAF between 1970 and 1977. Providing the background information that readers will require to understand the context in which these events occurred, separate thematic sections deal with the 1976 murder of Ulrike Meinhof in prison, the 1977 Stammheim murders, the extensive use of psychological operations and false-flag attacks to discredit the guerilla, the state's use of sensory deprivation torture and isolation wings, and the prisoners' resistance to this, through which they inspired their own supporters and others on the left to take the plunge into revolutionary action. With introductions by Russell Maroon Shoatz and Bill Dunne. (2009)

THE RED ARMY FACTION, A DOCUMENTARY HISTORY, VOLUME 2: DANCING WITH IMPERIALISM

ANDRE MONCOURT & J. SMITH EDS.
9781604860306 • 480 pp. • $26.95

This work includes the details of the Red Army Faction's operations, and its communiqués and texts, from 1978 up until its 1984 offensive. This was a period of regrouping and reorientation for the RAF, with its previous focus on freeing its prisoners replaced by an anti-NATO orientation. This was in response to the emergence of a new radical youth movement in the Federal Republic, the Autonomen, and an attempt to renew its ties to the radical left. The possibilities and perils of an armed underground organization relating to the broader movement are examined, and the RAF's approach is contrasted to the more fluid and flexible practice of the Revolutionary Cells. At the same time, the history of the 2nd of June Movement (2JM), an eclectic guerilla group with its roots in West Berlin, is also evaluated, especially in light of the split that led to some 2JM members officially disbanding the organization and rallying to the RAF. Finally, the RAF's relationship to the East German Stasi is examined, as is the abortive attempt by West Germany's liberal intelligentsia to defuse the armed struggle during Gerhard Baum's tenure as Minister of the Interior. With an introduction by Ward Churchill. (2013)

REMEMBERING THE ARMED STRUGGLE: LIFE WITH THE RED ARMY FACTION

MARGRIT SCHILLER • 9781629638737
239 pp. • $19.95

Former Red Army Faction political prisoner Margrit Schiller recounts the process through which she joined her generation's revolt in the 1960s, going from work with drug users to joining the antipsychiatry political organization the Socialist Patients' Collective and then the RAF. She tells of how she met and worked alongside the group's founding members, Ulrike Meinhof, Andreas Baader, Jan-Carl Raspe, Irmgard Möller, and Holger Meins; how she learned the details of the May Offensive and other actions while in her prison cell; about the struggles to defend human dignity in the most degraded of environments, and the relationships she forged with other women in prison. (2021)

SETTLERS: THE MYTHOLOGY OF THE WHITE PROLETARIAT FROM MAYFLOWER TO MODERN

J. SAKAI • 9781629630373 • 456 pp. • $20.00

Settlers exposes the fact that America's white citizenry have never supported themselves but have always resorted to exploitation and theft, culminating in acts of genocide to maintain their culture and way of life. As recounted in painful detail by Sakai, the United States has been built on the theft of Indigenous lands and of Afrikan labor, on the robbery of the northern third of Mexico, the colonization of Puerto Rico, and the expropriation of the Asian working class, with each of these crimes being accompanied by violence. This new edition includes "Cash & Genocide: The True Story of Japanese-American Reparations" and an interview with author J. Sakai by Ernesto Aguilar. (2014)

STAND UP STRUGGLE FORWARD: NEW AFRIKAN REVOLUTIONARY WRITINGS ON NATION, CLASS AND PATRIARCHY

SANYIKA SHAKUR • 9781894946469
208 pp. • $13.95

Firmly rooted in the New Afrikan Communist tradition, laying bare the deeper connections between racism, sexism, and homophobia and how these mental diseases relate to the ongoing capitalist (neo-)colonial catastrophe we remain trapped within. (2013)

STRIKE ONE TO EDUCATE ONE HUNDRED: THE RISE OF THE RED BRIGADES 1960S-1970S

CHRIS ARONSON BECK, REGGIE EMILIANA, LEE MORRIS, AND OLLIE PATTERSON • 9781894946988 • 296 PP. • $24.95

Today there are many books and countless papers and articles about the Red Brigades' history, but most are from a police and state point of view. Strike One is a unique and practically useful work, because it tells the other side, of innovative anticapitalism. It details how the spectre of urban guerrilla warfare grew at last out of the industrial centers of modern Italy, showing how this was a political project of a young working class layer that was fed up with reformism's lies. The authors, who were varied supporters who chose to remain anonymous due to Italy and NATO's draconian "anti-terrorist" laws, tell much of this story in the militants' own words: in translations of key political documents, news reports and communiqués. Indispensable. (2019)

THE STRUGGLE WITHIN: PRISONS, POLITICAL PRISONERS, AND MASS MOVEMENTS IN THE UNITED STATES

DAN BERGER • 9781604869552 • 128 pp. • $12.95

The Struggle Within is an accessible yet wide-ranging historical primer about how mass imprisonment has been a tool of repression deployed against diverse left-wing social movements over the last fifty years. Berger examines some of the most dynamic social movements across half a century: Black liberation, Puerto Rican independence, Native American sovereignty, Chicano radicalism, white antiracist and working-class mobilizations, pacifist and antinuclear campaigns, and earth liberation and animal rights. (2014)

TURNING MONEY INTO REBELLION: THE UNLIKELY STORY OF DENMARK'S REVOLUTIONARY BANK ROBBERS

ED. GABRIEL KUHN • 9781604863161
224 pp. • $20.00

One of the most captivating chapters from the European anti-imperialist milieu of the 1970s and '80s; the Blekingegade Group had emerged from a communist organization whose analysis of the metropolitan labor aristocracy led them to develop an illegal Third Worldist practice, sending millions of dollars acquired in spectacular heists to Third World liberation movements. (2014)

V.I. LENIN ON IMPERIALISM & OPPORTUNISM

V.I. LENIN • INTRODUCTION BY TORKIL LAUESEN
ISBN 9781894946940 • 191 PAGES • $13.00

The connection that Lenin posits between imperialism and opportunism—that is, the sacrifice of long-term socialist goals for short-term or sectional gains—is more pronounced than ever. Imperialism may, in many respects, have changed its economic mechanisms and its political form, but its content is fundamentally the same, namely, a transfer of value from the Global South to the Global North. (2019)

WHEN RACE BURNS CLASS: SETTLERS REVISITED

J. SAKAI • 9781894820264 • 32 pp. • $4.00

An interview with author J. Sakai about his groundbreaking work Settlers: Mythology of the White Proletariat, accompanied by Kuwasi Balagoon's essay "The Continuing Appeal of Imperialism." Sakai discusses how he came to write Settlers, the relationship of settlerism to racism, and between race and class, the prospects for organizing within the white working class, and of the rise of the far right. (2011)

THE WORKER ELITE: NOTES ON THE "LABOR ARISTOCRACY"

BROMMA • 9781894946575 • 88 pp. • $10.00

Revolutionaries often say that the working class holds the key to overthrowing capitalism. But "working class" is a very broad category—so broad that it can be used to justify a whole range of political agendas. The Worker Elite: Notes on the "Labor Aristocracy" breaks it all down, criticizing opportunists who minimize the role of privilege within the working class, while also challenging simplistic Third Worldist analyses. (2014)

KER SPL EBE DEB

Since 1998 Kersplebedeb has been an important source of radical literature and agit prop materials.

The project has a non-exclusive focus on anti-patriarchal and anti-imperialist politics, framed within an anticapitalist perspective. A special priority is given to writings regarding armed struggle in the metropole, the continuing struggles of political prisoners and prisoners of war, and the political economy of imperialism.

The Kersplebedeb website presents historical and contemporary writings by revolutionary thinkers from the anarchist and communist traditions.

Kersplebedeb can be contacted at:

Kersplebedeb
CP 63560 CCCP Van Horne
Montreal, Quebec
Canada
H3W 3H8

email: info@kersplebedeb.com
web: www.kersplebedeb.com
www.leftwingbooks.net

Kersplebedeb